T0373952

CONTENTS

INTRODUCTION

In 2008 I set out to examine the experience of evacuated Guernsey civilians, and to give these evacuees, who have largely been forgotten by historians, a voice. I was able to interview people in Guernsey, together with many that had remained in England after the war. I was also able to interview some who were young mothers during the evacuation, and their stories were particularly moving. Sadly a great many evacuees had passed away by the time I began my research, research which was very emotional and created close relationships with some of my interviewees. It also led to my involvement in a number of events which marked the seventieth anniversary of the evacuation in 2010, which changed my life completely.

I

COUNTDOWN TO EVACUATION

My childhood was left inside.
when I closed my bedroom door.
In the hall, distraught, father waits, mother weeps.
The dog unaware, wags his tail
and licks the tears from my face.

Reluctantly we speed to the harbour.
The smell of tobacco smoke on
father's jacket will remain with me.
On the ship we say goodbye, perhaps forever.
I feel empty like a shell.[1]

On 28 June 1940, at about 6.30 p.m., German aircraft appeared over the island of Guernsey. At the time Valerie Pales was helping her mother to harvest their potato crop, and recalls:

One plane broke away from the others and started machine-gunning our field, we could hear the bullets breaking panes of glass in our glasshouse and were worried that my father was in there, luckily he was in a brick-built shed. My mother hurried me to our house to shelter under the stairs. Father joined us and said that my mother and I would be safer in England, so they packed a few belongings into their car and drove to the harbour.

It was a savage raid, as the aircraft dropped bombs on the pier and town, then swooped down to machine-gun the streets around the harbour, apparently assuming that the tomato lorries lined up at the harbour contained ammunition. Most of the lorry drivers had crawled under their vehicles for shelter, and when the lorries were hit, they were trapped underneath. An RAF Air Ministry report noted a similar attack on the island of Jersey and listed the casualties as follows 'Jersey: 3 dead, Several wounded, Guernsey: 23 killed, 36 wounded.'[2]

Private Board of the St John's Ambulance Brigade arrived at the harbour a few minutes later:

> Everything was in chaos, the produce lorries had been transferred into a line of fire . . . our number 2 ambulance, the best one in the island, was against the kerb, every bit of glass smashed, and the sides and back doors riddled with shrapnel and bullet holes . . . one patient had been killed as he lay on the stretcher . . . the attendant was severely injured.

The only defence the island had at the time was a Lewis gun on the *Isle of Sark* mail boat, which had recently arrived to take evacuees to England. As the air raid commenced, evacuees were still boarding, and Mrs Trotter wrote later:

> We had just sat down in the lounge when we heard terrific explosions! 50 minutes of terror followed! I stayed with the children whilst my husband went up top to offer assistance with the Lewis gun. The boat shook and trembled but luckily was not hit. Our guns were the only protection the island had. I later came up to find tomato lorries ablaze on the harbour and some people had been killed.

The raid continued until about 8.00 p.m., at which point the *Sark*'s Captain Golding asked those around the jetty if they wished to board his boat. The Pales family boarded, along with many others who had suddenly decided to leave the island. The ship prepared to leave Guernsey at 10.00 p.m. with 647 passengers, 200 more than Captain Golding had originally planned to carry. Somehow Valerie Pales became separated from her mother, and as the boat started to pull away, she recalled:

> My mother was on the boat, screaming out that she had lost her child. Luckily somebody picked me up after the gangway had been pulled up, and managed to hand me over the ship's rail to my distraught mother. I believe I was the last child evacuee to leave Guernsey.

Valerie Pales.

In early 1940, the Channel Island of Guernsey was home to around 40,000 people, whose income came mostly from tourism, fishing, horticulture and agriculture. The island is about 30 miles from the French coast, and 70 miles from England's south coast. In 1940, the majority of Guernsey's residents were born there, but English people had been drawn to the warmer climate and the opportunities for agriculture. Loyal to the British crown since AD 933, the Channel Islands originally belonged to the Duchy of Normandy, but when William became King of England in 1066, he continued to rule the Channel Islands as Duke of Normandy. The mainland of Normandy was lost to England in the thirteenth century but the islands remained loyal to England's King John. A British governor had been living in Guernsey since 1486, and the British flag was flown on the island, together with the Guernsey flag. 'God Save the King' was Guernsey's national anthem too, and Joan Ozanne recalls, 'it was sung before every cinema and theatre show. The inhabitants perceived themselves, not just as residents of Guernsey, but also as British:

If there are two qualities upon which Channel Islanders pride themselves, they are their loyalty and their independence. These qualities they possess in common with all the British race.[3]

From the moment that Germany invaded France in May 1940, those living in the nearby Channel Islands of Guernsey, Jersey, Alderney and Sark were unsure whether their islands would be attacked or ignored by Hitler. However, in early June, as France began to fall, and British troops retreated to England, French refugees began to arrive in Guernsey's main harbour, St Peter Port. Fears arose that a German invasion might indeed take place, as the closeness of Guernsey to Cherbourg meant that the island was wide open to attack by German forces both by sea and by air. The Revd W.H. Milnes, the Principal of Elizabeth College, visited the Governor of Guernsey to express his fears that the island might be occupied, and to ask whether any plans were in hand for the evacuation of Guernsey's schoolchildren, stating later:

> Though some of those in authority doubted whether anything should be done, the Governor saw my point and it was agreed that the Procureur and I, should fly to London to arrange the evacuation of the schoolchildren in the Channel Isles.

However, the situation escalated to such a degree that no officials were able to leave the island for London. The Revd Mr Milnes began to assemble equipment for the evacuation of his pupils, realising that 'an evacuation across the sea was going to be a very different affair from an English evacuation from one county to another.' At the same time, the fate of the Channel Islands was being debated in London. On 11 June the British War Cabinet considered that Hitler might occupy the Channel Islands to 'strike a blow at our prestige by the temporary occupation of British territory.' Winston Churchill found it repugnant to abandon British territory which had been in the possession of the Crown since the Norman Conquest, and felt it ought to be possible 'by the use of our sea power, to prevent the invasion of the islands by the enemy.' However, the Vice Chief of Naval Staff advised Churchill that the equipment necessary for the defence of the Channel Islands was not available. The cabinet had two objections to the evacuation of *all* Channel Island civilians to England. The first was the probability of enemy air attacks on unprotected evacuation ships, the second was the thought that the inhabitants might not be willing to leave. After some deliberation, the cabinet finally decided:

> The Channel Islands are not of major strategic importance either to ourselves or the enemy . . . we recommend immediate consideration be given by the Ministry of Home Security . . . for the evacuation of all women and children on a voluntary and free basis.

On 16 June, the British Government ordered the removal of British troops from the Channel Islands, believing that they would be put to better use on the English coast. As troops began to leave the islands, this caused some despondency among the population. The government did not provide evacuation plans for the islanders at this stage, as they could not promise them any ships until the evacuation of British forces from France had been completed. On Monday 17 June, Guernsey's Education Council supported the evacuation of all schoolchildren, should such a course be recommended. On 18 June, the President of the Education Council invited Guernsey headteachers to an emergency meeting, to inform them that the evacuation of schoolchildren was a possibility. That same evening, the sound of guns and explosions on the French coast could be heard in Guernsey, causing some alarm, and the Revd Mr Milnes wrote:

We could hear the explosions from Cherbourg and other places on the French mainland . . . parents were getting very anxious and my telephone went day and night, so continuously, that I had to employ two helpers to take the calls.

On the morning of 19 June, as the headteachers met to discuss their plans, the bailiff, Victor Carey, arranged an emergency meeting with them. He told them that the British War Cabinet was discussing the position of the Channel Islands, and that the evacuation of schoolchildren would take place on a voluntary, rather than a compulsory, basis. Those present were pledged to secrecy for the time being, but a few hours later, news reached Victor Carey from the British Government that several evacuation ships would reach Guernsey the next day to commence the evacuation of the schoolchildren and their teachers. Guernsey teachers were quickly advised of the evacuation plans, and leaflets were printed for parents, to explain exactly what each child could take in the way of clothing and equipment. That same afternoon a free edition of the *Guernsey Star* informed parents that if they wished to send their children away the following morning, they should register at their child's school from 7.00 p.m. that very evening. Mothers with infants and men of military age also had the option to leave the island.

The Revd Mr Milnes assembled his Elizabeth College pupils and Ron Blicq recalls his solemn announcement:

Within a few days Guernsey almost certainly will be occupied by German troops. Consequently, starting tomorrow, the Government plans to bring a fleet of boats to the island to evacuate everyone who wishes to leave before the enemy arrives. I must make it clear that no one has to go. Your parents will tell you whether

GUERNSEY'S OLDEST NEWSPAPER

The ✸ Star.

ESTABLISHED 1813

"THE STAR" may be posted to Canada and Newfoundland at magazine rates. Registered at the G.P.O as a newspaper

CXXVI.—No. 146 WEDNESDAY, JUNE 19, 1940. GRATIS

ISLAND EVACUATION
ALL CHILDREN TO BE SENT TO MAINLAND TOMORROW
Mothers May Accompany Those Under School Age
REGISTRATION TONIGHT
WHOLE BAILIWICK TO BE DEMILITARISED
Strong Advice To Men Between 20 and 33

The Guernsey Star *evacuation notice.*

you are to stay or leave. And they will tell you their own plans . . . the College has to be ready to leave at any time after nine o'clock tomorrow.

Ironically several families had recently moved to the island, thinking that Guernsey would be safer than England. Several English boys were sent to Guernsey in late 1939. Thirteen-year-old Kenneth Cleal was sent from London to his father's family in Guernsey. His parents believed that the war would pass the island by and that Kenneth would be safer there. He attended the Boys' Grammar School and was evacuated with the school to the Oldham area in June 1940. Just a few months earlier, the Pales family had set up a horticultural business on the island.

Some families' decisions to evacuate may have been influenced by another article on the front page of the *Guernsey Star*, which advised islanders that:

Six boat loads of refugees reach St Peter Port; More French refugees, fleeing from the terror of German planes and troops arrived in Guernsey last night . . . there isn't a soul left in the town of Cherbourg . . . as we left, the docks were being blown sky high.

Winifred Best described the view as she had looked out towards the tiny island of Herm:

> The whole sky was black like the middle of the night! Mixed with this were flames, Cherbourg was on fire! By 4pm the whole island was in darkness, I will never forget it.

At the time, Jack Martel was in Guernsey on leave, having narrowly escaped Dunkirk where his helmet was dented by shrapnel while wading out to the boats to escape. His sister Marie recalls:

> Jack hurriedly brought in my clothes from the washing line and packed them into his kit bag. This later proved a problem, for on his arrival in Falmouth, he and his cousin, Alfred Digard, were arrested as suspected spies for 'being in uniform and travelling on a civilian boat', also 'being in possession of children's clothing'.

Guernsey parents now had just a few hours to make a crucial decision – whether or not to send their children away to England the next morning. Richard Adey was on the beach when he noticed his mother waving to him in an agitated manner:

> 'Quickly!' she said, 'Dad's brought the car and we have to go home immediately.' Now this in itself indicated a crisis, our car was not used lightly and without due thought, but today it seemed that the world and us with it had turned upside down. All the adults on the beach were talking in a hushed and serious manner.

Rachel Rabey heard her mother and aunt whispering throughout the night, then at breakfast:

> I was told that the school were going on holiday and I could go too. A little suitcase was packed, I still have it with my name hastily painted in white across the lid.

Paulette Tapp was living with her grandmother at the time, and one of the nuns from her school came to announce that the school was to be evacuated:

> If only you could imagine her sorrow, and also my aunty and uncle. She packed up my clothes crying. I was not really old enough to understand. I saw everybody crying, so I started to cry.

Some Guernsey parents were concerned for the safety of their daughters and Joanne James recalled 'my parents had heard stories of rape by German troops in Europe, and were too afraid to leave me in Guernsey so made the decision to let me go.' Therese Riochet found her mother in the kitchen, with a paper with instructions in her hand, and two labels with her name and address on them:

> I asked what they were for, and she answered, 'You are going to be evacuated with the school.' Then I asked her why, she said, 'You heard those guns last night didn't you . . . well they were at Cherbourg on the coast of France. The Germans are there and people say they are coming here to Guernsey.'

Some families did not actually see the newspaper report announcing the evacuation. Pamela Blunt's family knew nothing about the evacuation until an ice cream seller came round in his sidecar at 3.30 a.m., 'ringing a bell and telling us that the schools were to be evacuted that morning. We left home only a few hours later.'

In his book, *No Cause for Panic*, Brian Read pointed out that:

> There was widespread panic, several farmers slaughtered their cattle unnecessarily and thousands of parents drove to the local veterinary surgery to have their dogs and cats put to sleep.

Muriel Parsons family tried to catch their cat, Nippy, to give him to the vet, but Nippy lived up to his name and escaped over the garden wall. He later returned to the house where Muriel found him 'sitting in the kitchen, purring and looking pleased with himself – he was caught the next day and then he was – no more.' One little girl accompanied her mother to the vet, having been told that their cat was to be cared for while they were away. It was several years later when she realised why her mother had been crying as they had driven away from the vet's office. Mr Godfray recalled 'at the last moment, my friend, who was coming with us, drove off home to shoot his dog.' Others simply turned their animals loose as they left their homes, and Anne Misselke recalls:

> There were loose cows wandering about and a few cats and dogs . . . then there was a little kitten running about and suddenly two budgies flew overhead. Well, we had a budgie as well and a kitten, I was worried and said to mum 'if you go to England, Mummy, you aren't going to let Happy and Lucky out to fly about and walk about like that are you?'

Animals had recently been killed in England too – in late 1939 the animal-loving citizens of Britain, fearful of carpet bombing, evacuation and food shortages, had begun to put down their pets.[5] In addition, farmers had culled many of their animals as they were ordered to concentrate on growing more crops to feed the British public.

Many evacuees buried valuables in their gardens, houses were left abandoned with the keys still in the doors, and thousands went to the bank to try to draw out their money. There was a desperate rush to obtain suitcases, but the few shops which sold them soon ran out of stock. As a result, many evacuees left Guernsey with just a few possessions crammed into a pillowcase or a tomato basket. Between 20 and 28 June an estimated 17,000 people left Guernsey, but the first to leave were around 5,000 schoolchildren with their teachers and 500 adult helpers. The children's parents had received official instructions that:

> It will not be possible, on account of the danger of air raids, to permit masses of people to congregate at the habour, and accordingly, parents must say au revoir to their children at their homes or at their schools.

On the morning of 20 June, parents walked their children to the school gates where tearful farewells took place. Muriel Bougourd recalls:

> I remember we had to leave home very early and it was dark, my father took me to school on the back of his bike (no cars in those days) [and] we all had to meet at the school. We were then taken on buses down to the harbour. I remember the crowds and darkness, and although it was June my mother had put me in my winter coat and beret. I had a small suitcase; there wouldn't have been much room for more than a change of clothes. At the very last minute they realised that I had no comb – my hair was long, so my father gave me a small pocket comb.

Rhona Le Page recalls hugging her parents at the gates:

> They told me that I was just going for a day out with my school. Yet later, I was confused when two of my friends said that their mum had told them they were going away to England and that they themselves hoped to follow on the next available boat.

Some children saw the coming evacuation as an exciting event in their lives. Margaret Carberry was evacuated with her school, and her mother, and remembers packing her bag:

I think we probably thought it was a big adventure to be going on a boat trip to England; for us it was like going on a holiday and we had never been on a holiday before, I don't remember being worried about leaving Guernsey. That may have been because my mother was going to be with us.

The promised ships were late in arriving at the islands and Janice Rees recalled the long wait at the harbour for her boat:

First of all standing up holding our belongings, then we put our cases down, till we gradually sat on them. We sat in this attitude for so long that we broke the sides of our cases.

Some of the ships did not arrive and some children actually returned home again, which surprised and shocked their parents. Many could not bear to part with their children for a second time, so unpacked their suitcases and kept them at home. Others endured a very emotional evening, and had to repeat the walk to the school gates with their children the following morning. Arthur Trump was evacuated with the Castel School and recalled:

Although around 50 pupils were evacuated, many more should have gone. We assembled at the school two or three times but it was always cancelled because there were no boats available. By the time we left, half the people who were meant to go didn't turn up.

One headmaster noted in his diary that, when his school group reassembled, only 134 children arrived out of the 170 who had turned up the previous day. Isabel Ozanne recalls:

I was nine years old, an only child. My friends and teachers all left on buses to catch the boat, but my mum decided to take me back home. I left the next day in the care of two young mothers with babies and schoolchildren. I guess my parents thought that they would keep an eye on me.

Guernsey's Education Council noted later:

Throughout the evacuation we were greatly handicapped by parents changing their minds. Actually 755 teachers and helpers had registered at the Vale and Torteval Schools but there were many withdrawals at the last moment and we were able to put 76 Alderney children aboard the *Sheringham* in addition to the local schools.[6]

Captain James Bridson and evacuees on the SS Viking.

Second Officer Harry Kinley described his experiences as the children began to board the SS *Viking*:

> By 9 a.m. the children were arriving in great numbers and I will never forget the sight of those thousands of children lined up on the pier with their gas masks over their shoulders and carrying small cases. From the age of four to seventeen they came aboard, many of them in tears. It was hard to keep back our own tears I can tell you. We stopped counting the children after 1,800 and with the teachers and helpers, there must have been well over 2,000 on board.

The *Viking* was completely packed, with every cabin, corner and space filled with children, teachers and helpers. Ron Gould saw his father just before he went aboard, 'Dad gave me what he had in his pocket, which was a 10s note (50 pence today), and nice nearly new penknife.' Harry Kinley gave up his cabin to a dozen children and their Sunday school teacher. One mother gave her front door key to the chief officer, asking him to lock her front door if the ship went back to Guernsey because she had forgotten to do so. The captain of the SS *Haslemere* stated:

On arrival in Guernsey I was informed that I was required to leave as soon as possible with 350 children who had been on the quay since 0300 hours.

Numerous vessels, including ferry boats, mail boats, cattle boats and cargo boats evacuated children and adults to England. The SS *Whistable* picked up children from Jersey then proceeeded to Guernsey, where the captain noted:

Alarm at Guernsey appeared rather acute, and people were presenting themselves faster than they could be embarked. There were large numbers of cars left abandoned on the quay . . . we took on 340 people, 150 children and around the same number of women. The officers' quarters were reserved for the aged and infirm, invalids and nursing mothers.

Sir Geoffrey Rowland stated that as the evacuees left Guernsey, 'they were leaving, just hoping for the best, in a true British way.' As one ship parted from the quay, the national anthem was sung as the gap quickly widened between those on the shore. John Warren wrote to a relative in England to describe the events taking place in Guernsey:

The startling developments in the war situation are having a rather alarming effect on the islands. We are so close to France that no one can tell what may happen from one day to another. The authorities have ordered the evacuation of schoolchildren, and parents with young children are also being advised to leave as soon as possible . . . the islands are being demilitarised to prevent air attacks. I can tell you it has been an extraordinary experience as it has all happened so suddenly. Lots of people are leaving and the island already seems half empty!

Mrs Trotter noted that:

Banks still had their long queues, and one heard on every side the question – are you going? Some shop girls panicked and [went] off onto the boats with just their handbags and very little else. A baker's van man got the wind up, drove his van to the quay and walked on board, leaving the van with its load of bread to be removed by anyone who wished.

On 20 June, in an attempt to calm things down, the evacuation announcement was reissued in the *Star*, with the added comment that evacuation 'was not compulsory, but voluntary', and adding 'No cause for panic, Run on Banks must stop. Advice to carry on as usual'. The *Star* also produced posters bearing statements such as 'The Rumour that General Evacuation has been ordered is a

Lie'. However, someone else produced posters with slogans such as, 'Keep your Heads. Don't Be Yellow. Business as Usual', but these seem to have added to the confusion. They also appear to have caused friction between some who were leaving and some who were staying. Winifred Best recalled:

> I left with my mum and dad. We got to the harbour and lots of people were upset that there were posters up saying 'Don't be yellow, stay at home'.

Ted Hockey, the harbour signaller, heard officials persuading evacuees not to leave:

> They said that trade would carry on as usual, there would be no worry or trouble, and if it came to the worst, they would see that everybody got safely away. They had cars going round with posters, saying 'don't be yellow'. As a result of this, I saw one ship which could have carried 4,000 people and I doubt she carried more than 50!

As Mr Symons prepared to leave, he heard an official saying, 'Look at the rats leaving the sinking ship!' Yvonne Russell's mother and siblings had already left Guernsey so she 'decided to follow them to England, and to leave with my father, however, some people had decided to stay, and were calling those who wanted to go "cowards".'

Merle Roberts was a student teacher at Capelles Junior School, and wrote:

> The harbour was thronged with agitated people trying to decide what to do. The noise was terrific, with broadcasts telling people 'not to be yellow and not leave the island'. Some decided to go back home and take the consequences, others to stick to their decision to go.

Martin Le Page recalled:

> This was not the time for me to be faced with yellow posters, with black lettering which read 'Don't be yellow, stay at home' . . . how I longed to give the idiot who thought that one up a piece of my mind.

Some Guernsey and Jersey newspaper reports criticised the adult evacuees and said, 'If the people are going to be true to their traditions, they should go back to their homes so that they can follow their ordinary occupations.' Another referred to 'people scuttling away in an attempt to save their own skins.' One child heard adults talking about who was leaving:

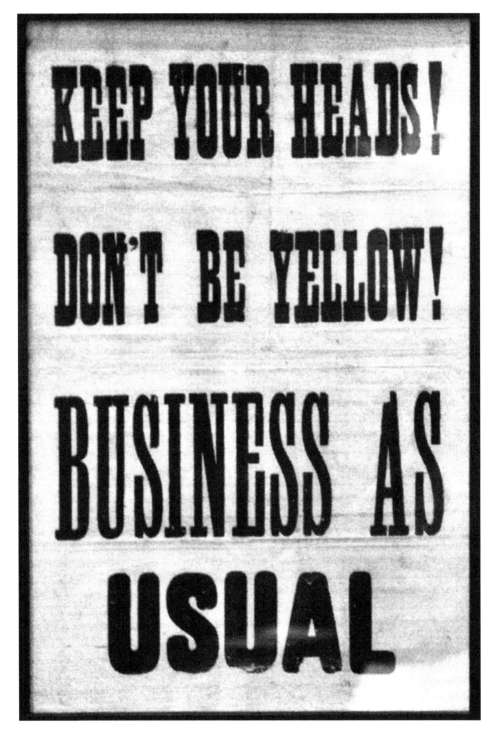

'Yellow' poster.

They would say 'so and so is leaving, they're yellow.' And I remember seeing Mr So and So a few days later and I looked at him and he wasn't yellow, he was a perfectly normal colour.

The evacuation of the schools gave thousands of young children the opportunity to escape, but interviews show that many older children remained on the island with their fathers, to look after the family home and business. Harold Le Page recalled:

My mum and sister left Guernsey on 22 June, but Dad wanted me to stay with him, I was nearly thirteen and he needed me there to help with the farm – his brother who helped him previously on the farm had gone to join the Army.

Only men of military age were permitted to leave on the first wave of official evacuation ships, although some men, and a number of complete families, managed to leave the island on other vessels. A number of Guernsey men and women who had been born in England left the island because they feared ill treatment from German forces if the occupation did take place.

Mothers and single women had to decide whether to offer to accompany the schools as helpers, or to remain behind. Mrs Ruth Alexandre wrote in her diary, 'News of demilitarisation of the island – we registered, chaos and confusion reigned, didn't know what to do, but was advised to go.' About 500 women left in this way, and their stories are particularly emotional. Reta Batiste left as a helper with the Forest School, and in her diary she described leaving her husband:

Wilf took our suitcases down to the Gouffre for us, his last words were 'I cannot bear to see you off', it was too much for him to bear, then we each went our way. It was a dreadful feeling, the whole party in the bus, waving, crying goodbye. The children were singing away not realising what it all meant.

Lorraine and Stephen Johns left with their four-month-old baby Elizabeth, and Violet Hatton left with her son Brian, aged six months. After her daughter had evacuated with her school, Olive Le Conte left with her baby, and wrote in her diary:

Margaret left at 3 a.m., I left with David in his Kari cot at 10.30 a.m. Osmond took me to the boat. Left my home clean and tidy, did not put anything away. Leaving my darling husband and home was terrible, am feeling broken hearted.

*Lorraine and Stephen Johns
with Elizabeth.*

Winnie Digard was pregnant when she boarded a ship with her young children:

> Whilst I was waiting for the bus to take us down to the ship, my baby quickened, and I fainted. Someone tied a ribbon around my arm to let people know that I was expecting. My suitcase was full and heavy with clothing for my children and a layette that my mother had bought for the new baby to wear when it was born.

Dorothy Taylor had given birth three weeks before the evacuation, and hurriedly had her daughter, Phyllis, christened in the minister's front room. Miriam Robilliard was in the middle of doing her weekly wash when her husband told her to leave for England with their two-year-old daughter, Margaret. Eva Le Page left Guernsey with her infant son, Anthony, and a bag which contained only nappies and feeding bottles. She had not wanted to leave Guernsey at all. She and her husband had argued tearfully throughout the night, but he had convinced Eva to leave Guernsey in order to protect herself and Anthony. Bert Le Page left the island to join the forces. Ron Gallienne's father promised he would follow his wife and son to England:

Margaret Robilliard.

Eva, Bert and Anthony Le Page.

My father came to say goodbye – he said he would take a later boat after looking after livestock but he didn't get away. My Aunt Linda also came to see us off, I remember Mum begging her to come with us, she too said 'next boat' – tug of war between her and Mum to let my cousin come with us, but to no avail.

Pamela Marchant recalled:

My father told my mum to leave and to take me and my sister with him. He said he would stay with grandmother and his parents and that if things got worse, they would all try to get onto a cargo boat later. They never got away.

A similar situation faced Molly Cowley:

A lot of people thought that we would only have to stay away from the island for a couple of months. Dad remained behind to look after our home, but then the Germans invaded the island and he could not join us in England. It was too late for him to get away.

Gavin Dorey's father owned his own boat, and felt that if enemy ships appeared on the horizon, it would be easy to make a last-minute getaway. After initially deciding to stay, Marie Martel's father decided to evacuate:

Dad received a phone call later that afternoon from a family friend, Captain Walsh, Master of the *Portelet,* a collier boat, who told him that if he was at St Sampson's Harbour by 6 p.m. he would take the whole family including Mum's unmarried sister Maggie, to England.

As they sailed to England, the evacuees endured rough Channel crossings as conditions were not ideal on most of the boats. Mike Dene sailed on a cargo boat which carried 300 people but was only licensed to carry 12. Evacuees were frequently crammed into airless cargo holds, or sat on the fully exposed decks. Dorothy Ogier travelled on the *Hantonia* which had recently been used to carry troops, and was smelly and dirty:

After it had steamed out of the harbour, some of the younger children started feeling sick and were crying for their mothers. Down in the hold where my class had been sent it was crammed with children. Many of the younger children were now curled up on the floor sleeping or sobbing. 'I'm supposed to look after Nunoos' I thought, 'I should go and find her,' but the teacher had warned us not to leave our class. I was worried, but eventually, exhausted, I fell asleep.

Winifred Best and her parents sailed on an old coal boat which had come direct from France:

> There wasn't a seat on board, and everything was black with coal soot. Lots of us sat in the hold. We got a couple of lifebelts for my dad to sit on, whilst we sat on boards.

Mrs Ruth Alexandre noted in her diary:

> Hours on a cattle boat, in the hold. Torrential rain about two o' clock so all had to go under cover where cattle had recently been landed. Everything full of coal dust, sat on suitcases and ate sandwiches, gave some to a poor family. Mrs Gardner and I climbed onto planks and tried to doze for a while, everything very dark and cold.

The women helpers came into their own, as they comforted the schoolchildren. Their diaries show that they dealt with numerous cases of seasickness among the children; in most cases there was nowhere for the vomit to go, except all over the floors. Janice Rees recalled how the children all around her were sick on the floor:

> All those who were sick, and I can assure you I was one of them, just had to lie on the floor, with life belts for pillows where the cattle are put. No one could believe or imagine what it was like. Some people fainted and had to be watched carefully.

Mary Champion wrote later:

> We had no warm clothing, the journey in a cattle boat was rough and cold, toilet facilities were basic, and we were sitting on sheets in the dirty hold. The crossing was awful and I looked after 8 children. I remember helping one child to vomit, and then both of us slid around in it on the floor.

Winnie Digard recalled, 'The journey was awful and cramped. I was seasick and another mother helped me to look after my children,' and Marian Luscombe wrote, 'my mother spent the whole journey tending children who fell ill as there were few mothers aboard our boat.'

Some of the male passengers spent their time liaising with the ship's crews to find out about the progress of the journey, or trying to obtain food and drink for the evacuees. Gavin Dorey sailed on the *Batavia IV* and while chatting to the crew, discovered that the boat had been to Dunkirk four times to rescue troops 'and there were several rows of machine gun bullet holes in the wooden deck to substantiate the story'. Bob Gill found it a very exciting experience as he had never been to the mainland before – 'our boat bore the smell of cattle, but I had a great time as I spent the whole journey with the wireless operator.' Ted Hamel and his family sailed on the *Antwerp,* and he wrote later, 'We would have given the earth for a cup of tea. I set off in search and received a saucepan half filled with water.' Maureen Sherwin received a cup of tea from the ship's stoker – 'he handed me his mug which was all black and grimy, it was the best cup of tea I have ever tasted!' Michael and Peter Rose sailed on the *Princess Astrid,* and noticed that the ship had two large holes in its superstructure, one on the port side and one on the starboard:

> We asked how these came about and were told that it had been at Dunkirk evacuating our troops, when a shell passed right through the ship apparently without having exploded!

Bernard Le Cocq recalls that Barclays bank needed someone to carry several thousand pounds of gold coin to England, so that German invaders would not get their hands on it. Roy Hill, a senior employee, had already sent his wife and children to England, so he was chosen to carry the gold. He spent an uncomfortable night 'standing on deck with his precious and weighty burden held securely between his feet.'[7]

The evacuation ships reached Weymouth where they often sat for hours, waiting for permission to disembark. Lawrie Ozanne recalled:

> As we approached Weymouth, another ship some distance away must have hit a mine and it was in the process of sinking. I remembered what my father had said, 'Look after the little ones', and I put my arms around Joan and David and wondered what I would be able to do if the same thing happened to us.

Amy Morse sailed on the *Courier* with her children Betty and Peter, and later she wrote a letter to her husband Bill, stating:

> At Weymouth it was raining while we were waiting, the boat was pretty hot, full of people, soaking wet babies, sick people and smells . . . we could have done with our gas masks on!

Steve Duquemin was with the Elizabeth College boys on the Dutch cattle boat *Batavia IV* and recalled, 'there was a flurry of activity, sirens sounded, naval ships sent signals to our boat by Aldis lamp. We waited several hours before we left the *Batavia*.' Len Robilliard noticed soldiers, who were stationed on a coastal gun at the entrance to Weymouth, running towards them, cheering and waving their caps at the boys. Winifred Best had never seen so many boats in her life:

> Hundreds of all shapes and sizes, from all different countries, waiting to dock. I saw other Guernsey evacuation boats and people started calling to us 'Have you seen so and so?' or 'Have you got so and so on board?' Our boat got priority to dock because we were a hospital ship. They took the patients and pregnant women off, then we tried to get father off because of his bad leg, but they wouldn't allow it. There was nothing on board to eat, and we evacuees had to sleep on board all night.

Winifred and her group disembarked the next morning, and were immediately approached by French interpreters:

> They didn't think we could speak English. Another person said 'We thought you'd all be in grass skirts,' and that upset us all, I can tell you!

Miss Dorey was told that the WVS 'were surprised to find that the colour of our skin was white, as they thought the Channel Islands were off the African coast.'[8]

After disembarking, the evacuees were quickly formed into long crocodiles and led away from the quayside into the Pavilion Theatre where they received refreshments and registered their personal details. Catherine Deacon was a Weymouth teacher who had come along to assist the evacuees, and she described the confusion that surrounded their arrival:

> Schoolchildren and teachers were brought in and I had to get the particulars down of each one. Their baggage and the children's food was left on the quay side, it often went missing as did their children. Children that were evacuated with their schools, separated from their mothers, were in the school hall.

The evacuees were then given a brief medical inspection and Gavin Dorey recalled that they were examined quite quickly:

> Goodness knows what they were trying to detect, but perhaps, as refugees from a distant land we were under automatic suspicion of having exotic diseases like leprosy or beri beri.

Anne Misselke remembers:

> You had to go and form a queue, so many children at each table and they
> looked into your eyes, in your ears, up your nose, down your throat. If you
> had any spots or anything, they gave you a pink label and you had to go out
> one way. So if you were fit they gave you a white label and you went out the
> other way.

Hazel Hall still possesses the medical label that was tied to her coat which stated
'NAD' – Nothing abnormal detected. Sadly, eleven-year-old Sylvia Burford
was not so lucky, being the one casualty of the Channel crossing. Sylvia was
evacuated with her school, while her mother and her sister, Polly, left on a
different ship. Just before the evacuation, Sylvia had undergone a tonsillectomy.
Polly recalls:

Hazel Hall's medical label.

Unfortunately Sylvia was very ill after the operation and should never have been moved to go on such a hazardous journey. She died on the boat just before reaching Weymouth. No sooner had my mother and I arrived at her parents in Rugby than the police came with the sad news about Sylvia. Mum returned to Weymouth with her father, for identification and burial.

Winifred Best recalled:

They asked us if we had friends or family in England, and if you did, they gave you a railway ticket to get you there and gave you directions. If you had nowhere to go, you were grouped together and taken to the railway station with lots of others.

Miss Grace Fry travelled as a helper with Vauvert School, and as her group were registering at Weymouth, an air raid began. She recalled:

My group of children and I were pushed out of the building and onto a bus, then to my horror, the driver locked the door and disappeared . . . the children had been sick and all smelt to high heaven, and were dropping off the bus seats in the dark because they were tired. We were there for about an hour or so. I had given up and thought, 'Well, this is the end, if a bomb falls on us, I hope it happens quickly!' Then the driver unlocked the door and said 'Out!' I had to feel with my foot under the seats in the dark to check whether I had all the children or not.[9]

A report written by St John Ambulance gave the total number of Channel Island evacuees who arrived in Weymouth as 23,743, and recorded astonishment at the arrival of so many children accompanied only by their teachers. Catherine Deacon recalled:

The mums were very distressed as they were brought in, but all their baggage was left on the quayside. There was a lot of confusion about who went where.

Some brothers and sisters were separated, and others lost the few possessions that they had. Janice Rees recalled that children that were still being ill were kept in Weymouth, 'that is where we all lost each other, we all got separated from our groups and children lost their mothers.'

Gladys Merrien was searching for her husband Jack, who had promised that he would follow her on the next boat. However, as another group of Guernsey evacuees disembarked, one spotted Gladys and told her that Jack had decided to stay in Guernsey for the time being. Beryl Merrien recalls:

Miriam Robilliard and her daughter Margaret.

This friend told Mum that Dad was going to stay in Guernsey to try to stick it out, and that he would get on a boat if it got really bad there. He wanted to keep the house and business together until there was any sign of Germans arriving. Also at the time, lots of the dogs in the island were being shot. Dad had a horse called Laddie, and he was reluctant to leave the horse as he would have to shoot it. So Mum agreed for us to get onto the next train from Weymouth and not wait for Dad any longer. We didn't hear from him again for fifteen months.

The Guernsey men who were of military age were dealt with separately. Raymond Carre fully expected to be called into the forces at Weymouth, but was advised that this was not compulsory for Channel Islanders, although they could volunteer if they so wished. Clem Brehaut was eighteen when he reached Weymouth on a tomato boat containing young men and fathers. Some planned to join up, while others were English-born and felt they would be safer in England. Many were also hoping to locate their wives and children who had evacuated on earlier boats. Clem recalls:

An order came, all men between 19 and 37 must line up on the right-hand side. The rest were sent elsewhere. We on the right were marched to the White Ensign Hotel, given a meal and a bed for the night. In the morning we were taken to the Registration office for the forces. [We were] all given a medical exam and told if fit or not fit. I told the officer that I wanted to find my family first to check that they were safe, before I joined up as they had arrived in England three days beforehand. I was then told we were going to be put on trains 'up north', destination unknown. I ended up in Glasgow and it took me 6 weeks to trace my family who had ended up in Stockport!

Between 8,000 and 10,000 islanders joined the British forces, even though it was not compulsory for them to do so. Some failed their medical inspections, such as Joe Le Page, who had a slight loss of hearing in one ear. As a result, many of these men undertook essential war work in England – Joe Le Page found work at Fairey Aviation, where a number of Guernsey evacuees worked throughout the war.

Because the south coast was experiencing air raids, the carefully prepared evacuation plans and train timetables now became useless. As the Channel Islanders arrived in Weymouth, English children were being evacuated away from Southampton and Portsmouth. The Channel Islanders needed to be quickly moved away from Weymouth by train, and only the Great Western and Western Divisions of the Southern Railway could be used as other lines were needed for military operations. For these reasons, the Ministry of

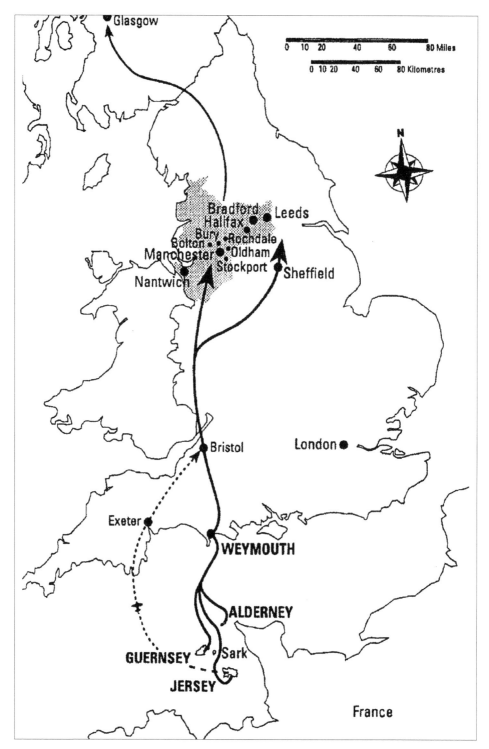

The main evacuation routes. (Image reproduced from No Cause for Panic: Channel Island Refugees 1940–45 *by Brian Ahier Read, Seaflower Books, 1995)*

Health decided to send the majority of the evacuees to three areas that had been designated as 'neutral areas' in northern England – factory towns in Lancashire, Cheshire and the West Riding of Yorkshire. Accommodation had previously been earmarked for Belgian refugees that had not yet arrived. The Guernsey evacuees were taken to Weymouth railway station, but most had never seen a steam train before and there was a mixture of excitement and fear. Hazel Knowles recalled:

> For the first time we saw a train. It was quite a frightening sight to see this huge monster with clouds of steam hissing from it. We then set out on a journey which seemed to take forever.

Sheila De la Mare recalls, 'My friends and I were terrified! We had to be pushed onto the train by our teachers!' One teacher, Grace Fry, found herself on the station platform surrounded by pupils from Vauvert School. Many were exhausted and she had made them hold onto her coat so that they would not become separated from her:

> I was carrying one child who was too sick to walk, plus my own small suitcase. Young soldiers began to push the children onto a train, then suddenly this big Major came out of the darkness, and said, 'Madam will you go on with your children?!' and I said 'But where?' Well, the train started to move, and a young Lieutenant came running down the platform, grabbed my hand and said 'Can you run?' and we set off at a terrific lick . . . a steward appeared in a white coat, at the open train door, and this young soldier pushed me into his arms, and then off we went.

Few evacuees were given any idea of their final destinations, despite the efforts of the teachers to obtain information. Beryl Merrien recalled:

> We had no idea where we were going. All the stations had their names removed so we kept calling out of the window 'where are we?' but no one on the platform would tell us. We eventually ended up in Glasgow.

However, one Guernsey teacher, Alec Rose, repeatedly asked the guard about their destination, and was eventually told, 'You're going to Oldham . . . and God help you! The guard was referring to a town of coal pits and slag heaps'. Those who managed to peep through the blackout curtains during the journey saw unfamiliar sights such as rivers and wide roads, and Rose Duquemin saw:

Strange sights such as black cows, we had only seen the golden Guernsey cows before . . . another sight was fields full of pigs . . . the only pigs I had seen before lived in stone pigsties, also the fields were so big compared with our little Guernsey fields.

The crowded trains travelled overnight, with frequent stops in railway tunnels, and only a handful of evacuees recall any stops being made to obtain food or water. Sheila Whipp recalled that sandwiches and soup were passed to the children through the train window when her train stopped at one station. Eva Le Page had her baby's enamel chamber pot with her, and when the train stopped at a station, a lady borrowed the pot and had it filled with tea on the station platform! At the end of their train journey, two long days after they had left Guernsey, some evacuees found themselves as far north as Glasgow, while the majority arrived in industrial towns in northern England such as Stockport, Bury, Oldham, Wigan, Halifax, Burnley and Bradford.

Evacuees who had friends or relatives in England faced an equally fraught journey to their final destinations. Most had never used a railway station before and had little or no knowledge of the geography of mainland Britain. Winifred Best and her parents had friends living in Blackpool:

> We were given train tickets to Blackpool but my dad had previously had a stroke, and had to drag one leg. We had to change trains at Bath and Preston. Can you imagine, we had no idea about railway stations, and crossing over the platforms was so hard for my poor old dad, with going up and down all the stairs to cross the platforms. My mum kept saying 'Come on!' as she was worried that we would miss the next train. The same panic stations at Preston too!

Back in Guernsey many people were still wondering if they should follow their family members to England, or stay behind. On 26 June, Jack De Garis received a letter and telegram from his evacuated wife, Mary, confirming that she and the rest of the family had arrived safely in England. He immediately wrote a letter to her:

> My very dear Mary . . . we were overjoyed to receive your letter and telegram . . . we have decided to stay for the time being. Keep looking up, there will be an end to all of this, one of these days, perhaps sooner than we dare expect. With love and kisses to you all . . . Your darling Jack.

Reginald Biddle, a Jersey man, was the dock and marine manager at Southampton at the time. On 28 June he learned of the German air attacks on Guernsey and Jersey, and made strenuous efforts to send more ships to the islands to collect evacuees. However, he received a telephone call from the Bailiff of Jersey which said in effect, 'No further evacuation is contemplated from either Jersey or Guernsey.' As a result, no further ships left England to collect evacuees from the Channel Islands. On 20 June the Guernsey evacuation had begun, and by 28 June an estimated 17,000 people had left for England. On 30 June, the island was occupied by German forces and thousands of people's lives were changed forever.

NOTES

1   Ozanne family papers, evacuation poem by Joan Ozanne.

2   RAF Museum, London, Air Ministry Report 29 June 1940.

3   *Nos Isles: A Symposium on the Channel Islands* (Channel Island Study Group: Middlesex, 1944), p. 3

4   The National Archives, ref. CAB/65/7/67 Cabinet War Room Memorandum, 19 June 1940, and ref. CAB/66/8/27, Cabinet War Room Memorandum, 11 June 1940.

5   Stephen Poliakoff, *History Today*, December 2009, p. 69.

6   Minutes of a Guernsey Education Council Meeting held on 28 June 1940, p. 2, Le Pelley papers.

7   Barclays Bank Archive, Manchester, *History of Barclays Bank: The Balance Sheet Dissected*, p. 55.

8   Second World War Experience Centre, interview with Mrs J. Glanville (née Dorey), 2001.

9   Guernsey Retired Teachers Association, interview with Miss Grace Fry.

2

FINDING A NEW HOME

> There were rivers and canals, viaducts, trains and noisy
> railway stations, cotton mills belching black smoke into the air,
> and coating everything with a dark grey dust, and the women
> wrapped in shawls who looked pale as if they never saw the sun.[1]

The majority of the Guernsey evacuees arrived in northern England and were shocked by the contrast between their rural island and the industrial landscape. They remember their first glimpses of smoking chimneys, terraced houses and factories. Bob Gill arrived in Oldham where he saw 'tripe in a butcher's window, the people were very friendly, but the clogs and shawls and mills were very unfamiliar and different'. Lawson Allez similarly recalled that 'people were very friendly but everywhere seemed so noisy after living on a quiet island'. Ron Gould arrived in Eccles, Manchester, and thought he was seeing things when:

> A large cargo ship many times larger than our mailboats, went steaming by, 40 miles from any sea. I soon found out that the Manchester Ship Canal was the reason for this!

Many evacuees visited the public baths, and John Le Brun recalls that during these excursions, 'we got our first real look at the industrial landscape which differed so much to our island home.' Molly Cowley was amazed to see trains, trams, and wide roads with two or three lanes!', while Richard Adey saw his first double-decker bus:

To me, it looked like there were two buses, one on top of the other! But there was no driver in the top one. It was a little frightening, going along, high up in the air, and hoping that the driver in the bus underneath knew where the top part wanted to go!

Robert Langlois was fascinated by the 27-arched, 34-metre-high brick railway viaduct in Stockport and drew several pictures of it, which he still has today.

When Ted Hamel was asked by locals what he thought of Bradford, he wrote later:

> I just couldn't tell these kind folk that I thought I'd been dropped in the Black Hole of Calcutta could I? So I compromised. I said that I wasn't thrilled at living in a city, but the wonderful welcome we had all received in Bradford made up for being so far from home.

Evacuees were horrified by the 'smog' – a mixture of fog and the coal smoke that poured from hundreds of house and factory chimneys. Len Robilliard remembers trying to get home on his bicycle, 'I could hardly see my hand in front of my face and walked past my own street three times.' Muriel Parsons noted in her diary, 'Thick fog. I led a string of cars to Cheadle. Only just managed to find the way myself!' Joan Wilson recalled being caught in the smog for the very first time:

Robert Langlois' drawing of Stockport viaduct.

Guernsey evacuees in Bradford.

I wondered what on earth had happened, it was only 3 o'clock in the afternoon . . . a bus appeared out of the darkness as I crossed the main road, and nearly hit me. I was glad to reach home!

Almost every evacuee interviewed missed Guernsey's beautiful coast and sea, and Muriel Bougourd recalls:

In Bradford there was no sea, and I just couldn't understand that. When we approached a moor I could see a blue haze which I was convinced was the sea, and I started to run towards it. My mother had to run after me and bring me back. What I could see was the heather at the start of the moor.

Council officials in northern towns had received very little notice of the evacuees' actual arrival. However, because they had been expecting refugees from Belgium and Holland, they were able to respond quickly to the imminent arrival of the Channel Islanders. On 20 June 1940, Bury officials were told that Channel Island evacuees were coming, but there was no warning that the majority would be children and teachers, and mothers and infants. Bury Council advised volunteers that a large number of British evacuees were coming to Bury, and issued them with supplies of soup, tea, coffee and blankets in readiness.[2] Stockport officials received only a few hours' notice of the arrival of Channel Island evacuees, yet hundreds of local children had recently been evacuated from Stockport to Canada for safety. The *Stockport Advertiser* announced the arrival of the Channel Islanders as follows:

1,200 EVACUEES ARRIVE IN STOCKPORT
Billeted in Public Buildings

The young evacuees after their first breakfast in Stockport, showing them with toys and books sent for them by local inhabitants. Th photograph was taken in the Edward Street entrance of the Town Hall.   ("Advertiser" Staff Photo

Evacuees at Stockport Town Hall. (Courtesy of Stockport Express)

The first warning was that a train would arrive at 3 a.m. Efforts were made to get as many voluntary workers there as possible. Some evacuees did not even know what day it was, so long had they been on their way by sea and land. Most of the adults were sad eyed and full of determination to endure anything to beat 'that beast' (meaning Hitler, of course).

Public buildings were turned into reception centres, including Stockport Sunday School, the Masonic Guildhall, and the enormous ballroom of Stockport Town Hall. Marian Greenhalgh was a Girl Guide at the time and remembers being taken to the town hall to help the evacuees:

I remember going up the marble staircase, picking our way through all the women and children sitting on the stairs . We spent our time mixing feeds for the babies and nursing them whilst their mothers went for a wash, etc. We played with the young children and read to them, to stop them crying. I can still see those wretched mothers looking so frightened.

Some evacuees were sent to the Davenport Methodist Church, where Yvonne Bristol recalls:

> They were expecting lots of children, and we were groups of all ages, mothers etc., so that caused them a bit of confusion, but they seemed to cope after a few hours.

Ted Hamel arrived in Bradford, where, 'later that day, cups of milk were brought in for the younger children. I had the feeling that children in such numbers had not been expected.'

Joan Prout recalled her first breakfast in Burnley which consisted of tripe and milk, 'I will never forget it, it made me sick!'

During these first few days, some evacuees managed to communicate with family and friends in Guernsey. Amy Morse wrote to her family, ending her letter with the words:

> Well old darlings, if you are there, write or wire, or telephone as soon as possible, we are cut off for news, we meet people (Guernsey) in streets and stop and ask for news, but none to satisfy us. God bless you all and keep you safe, Your loving wife and children, Amy, Betty and Peter.

Len Robilliard received a letter from his mother which included the words:

> You will see that we are still home and not leaving yet until things go bad . . . a good many houses are empty round this way. Let me know all about yourselves, I shall send you a few stamps next time I write.

Rachel Rabey received a letter from her aunt which asked her to be a good girl and to say her prayers for her family in Guernsey. Beryl Merrien recalled 'for the first few days we were able to telephone my father in Guernsey, who told us that there was no sign of any Germans.' However, the evacuees then received the shocking news that, on 28 June, Guernsey had been bombed by Germany. Mrs Reta Le Poidevin was in a church hall with 400 other evacuees when she heard the news, and people were in tears all around her as they wondered whether their families were alive or dead. Reta recalled, 'it was announced that there would be a service held in the adjoining church for us. The Minister was a kind and sympathetic man and the service was comforting and most impressive.'

Mrs Johns had been evacuated with her baby Elizabeth, and on 29 June she received the following telegram from her parents in Guernsey, 'Guernsey bombed last night. Many casualties. Staying here'. That evening, one of the school helpers, Muriel Parsons, wrote in her diary:

25ᵗ.6.40.

My darling little Rachel.
        What a lucky little
girl you are to be away
with all your little
school friends. I am
sure you are going to
be very happy and I
know you will be
a good girl and do
everything you are told
Don't forget to say
Gentle Jesus every night

and God bless Mummie
Daddy and little Jane
Auntie Ella will
think of you every
day, and will
write as often as I
can —
God bless you my
precious darling
Lots of love and
Kisses from
        Auntie Ella

I will write again soon
and send you some

Rachel Rabey's letter.

For the past half hour I have been sitting on my camp bed in a public hall, thinking. So much has happened during the past week that we are feeling somewhat dazed. We have laughed at our plight and helped each other to see the funny side, but deep down inside ourselves, we are very sad, and more than a little lost.

When the evacuees heard the dreadful news that the Channel Islands had been occupied by German forces on 30 June, they realised that they might have to stay in England for some time. However, the reception centres were clearly unsuitable for a long-term stay. The sanitary arrangements were inadequate, and the evacuees slept on makeshift pallets, in very close proximity, which meant that infectious diseases quickly spread among the children. The Elizabeth College boys lived above the Co-operative store in Oldham where toilet facilities were inadequate. Gavin Dorey recalled, 'we slept on mattresses arranged in rows on the floor, having our sleep interrupted at night by air raids.' Stockport Sunday School received over 200 evacuees from Guernsey and Jersey on 22 and 23 June 1940, and was the largest Sunday school in the world, containing one hundred rooms, and beautiful stained-glass windows, one of which is still preserved in the Stockport Story Museum. However, the only washing facilities were the sinks in the toilets. Mavis Brown recalled 'we

Elizabeth College boys at the Oldham Co-operative store.

lived for three weeks, sleeping on old mattresses and when we left, we found that we had lice and fleas'.

The Women's Royal Voluntary Service (WRVS) continued to search for more permanent accommodation for the evacuees. The *Stockport Advertiser* reported that house-to-house canvassing had taken place locally to find more homes for Channel Islanders. In Wigan, housewives were interviewed to find out who would take in an evacuee voluntarily, or for a billeting allowance. The allowance varied according to the age and number of evacuees in a household. For a child under the age of eight the rate was 8*s* 6*d* per week, while anyone billeting a mother would receive 15*s* per week.[3] In Bury, eighty teachers and pupils were quickly placed in empty houses in the newly completed Chesham Fold Council Estate. Each adult was provided with a leaflet containing basic information on local shops, employment, rationing and national assistance payments. Student teacher Dorothy Cope wrote, 'the schoolchildren were divided into groups of six and allocated a house each . . . there were three bedrooms in ours so it wasn't too crowded for us. I still remember the address, 72 Goldfinch Drive.'

Irene Moss shared a bedroom with her teacher, Miss Ninnim, stating, 'it must have been uncomfortable for my teacher to have to share my bedroom. I was of course on my best behaviour at all times!'

Before 1940, most English people had little knowledge of the Channel Islands, as foreign holidays were rare. The only references to Guernsey in pre-war newspapers related to tourism, Guernsey cattle breeding, Guernsey milk or the 3,000 packages of tomatoes that were exported to England every year. However, in June 1940, the arrival of thousands of evacuees from a British territory which had been invaded by Nazi Germany brought the reality of 'invasion' to Britain's doorstep. For months, the press had been discussing the invasion of Britain. In January 1940 the *Observer* had warned readers:

> For the Nazis, Britain is the enemy . . . they will not fall without attempting some desperate stroke . . . they must attempt their worst against this nation and this empire in the next six or seven months, or their regime must fall.

On 26 June 1940, *The Times* had stated:

> The whole German press this morning announced that a campaign of annihilation against England was about to be unleashed . . . in all cafés and places of amusement, crowds sing repeatedly the German war song – we are sailing for England!

From the moment the Channel Island evacuees set foot in England, their plight, and later, the occupation of their islands, filled the national and local press:

> First to come were the youngest tots. With dolls in their arms and their possessions in pathetic bundles, they came off the boats. A schoolmaster told us 'We were packed like herrings. The children had behaved like true Britishers and so had their parents who were left behind.'

A Bradford newspaper told readers 'the evacuees had to leave the Channel Islands hurriedly. One little boy was brought away at the last moment in a banana box.'

The Times deplored the occupation of Guernsey, 'the last remnants of the Duchy of Normandy to belong to the British Crown.' The *Manchester Guardian* called the evacuees 'Britons, our own people, who have sent thousands of volunteers to join the fighting forces.' One evacuee told the press, 'The Channel Islander of today is as much a countryman of the British Isles as the Welshman or the Scot, and quite as proud of it.' A number of evacuees sent reports to the press to provide local people with information about their island home. A Guernsey man in Bradford stated:

> I was told that if I remained in Guernsey, I must not raise a hand against any German. Well, you don't expect a Britisher to stay and not raise a hand against the invader, do you? So I decided to come here.

Newspaper reports describing the evacuees often included photographs of the children, gaining sympathy from the public and reminding adults of the stressful events surrounding the evacuation of their own children to the countryside in September 1939. The *Stockport Advertiser* showed Guernsey youngsters playing with the toys and books that had been given to them by local people. A Cheshire newspaper showed evacuees arriving in Disley, Cheshire, but the main focus of the picture is a pretty blonde infant (Rosalind Brelsford) in her mother's arms, and two small boys who are carrying small wicker tomato baskets. One reporter who helped circulate these photographs was Victor Lewis. Born in Guernsey, Victor was news editor of Manchester's *Daily Sketch* during the war. He wanted people to appreciate the unfortunate situation of the evacuees, so he interviewed and photographed the children, and passed the images to other newspapers. He even managed to get an article into the *Guernsey Star*, just before the German invasion of the island, to let parents know that their children had arrived safely:

> This is a message to the mothers and fathers of Guernsey children, who are now getting acclimatised to a temporary new life in the reception areas to which they have been sent in the North of England. These youngsters are safe and happy . . . the hospitable people of Lancashire have thrown open their homes wide to them.[4]

Guernsey evacuees arriving in Disley.

Lindsey, Derek and Jean Holmes.

It is clear from interviews with many of the evacuees that local people welcomed them into the community. Peter Ninnim and Derek Holmes' families moved into the same street in Stockport, where the Holmes family found rooms at the back of a hairdresser's shop – 'people were very friendly to us, and luckily, my father, who was a barber, was given a job for the duration of the war.' Peter Ninnim's family moved into an empty wool shop, and were touched by the welcome from local people:

> I cannot thank the people of Stockport enough for taking us into their community. In Edgeley, they were wonderful. We depended on the kindness of strangers many a time.

Mary Ingleton was living in Cheshire at the time:

> We heard that all these poor children had arrived and that the Nazis were on their island. We went along with presents for them, although we had little money to spare in those days.

Horsforth residents remember the arrival of around 400 Guernsey evacuees in their area, and local children immediately donated books and toys to the Guernsey children. Betty Lax recalled, 'On arrival we were asked to give one of our favourite toys as a welcome. I gave one of my favourite dolls!'[5] The Brayshay family gave a Guernsey family their gramophone as a gift, while Barbara West's family took in two Guernsey sisters, and she was delighted because, as an only child, she had always wanted sisters. She was delighted to share all her toys and dolls with them.

Anne Martins recalls, 'People brought us books and toys because they knew that our mums and dads wouldn't be able to send us anything.' Len Robilliard was standing outside his reception centre when 'a policeman came along and handed me a ten shilling note, a lot of money in 1940, and told me to use it to buy sweets for the children.' When the Guernsey children strolled around the streets of Bury, Irene Moss recalls:

> People used to stop and ask us 'Are you those evacuees?' and when we said 'Yes' they gave us pennies for sweets. They said that they had read all about us in the papers. They were so very kind to us. I will never forget that! One person even asked me for my autograph!

Paulette Tapp recalls a shopping trip when, 'one of our boys went to buy a book that cost 2s. When they realised he was a Guernsey evacuee they let him have it for 1s.' Raymond Le Page recalled many acts of kindness in Oldham:

> Upon the news of the bombing of our island I was filled with shock and anxiety for my family . . . but I can give the Oldham people nothing but my thanks. Their generosity to us boys, strangers, is a cause for gratitude for all who are passing through their hospitable town.

Entertainment was arranged for the children in many of the towns. Groups of children in Stockport were given free admission to the cinema, while Len Robilliard remembers that the evacuees were invited to garden parties, and a day out at Belle Vue, Manchester. In Oldham, John Laine recalls that the boys were given free entry into the cinema, football matches, and the swimming baths. Frank Le Messurier wrote to his sister telling her of the free concerts he had seen and his visits to the local baths, adding:

> We also went to a concert . . . [and] we saw a German prison camp that used to be a spinning factory. We have been to the pictures too and seen *Mutiny on the Bounty*.

In Bury the Scala, Hippodrome and Odeon cinemas offered the children free entry to the cinema each Saturday. Local firms sent gifts of food and fruit to the evacuees, and employees at the Bury Felt Manufacturing Company made 60 free mattresses for some of the children, unpaid, during their lunch hours.

Despite the newspaper reports which described the Guernsey evacuees as British, a number of English people still assumed they were 'foreign'. Tony Ozanne recalls that people 'were probably a bit more reserved with us initially because we were to them "refugees" and they were not sure what we were like.' Ruth Alexandre wrote in her diary, 'I told the girls at the Co-op we were from Guernsey, and was surprised to hear them say "Fancy! And you speak perfect English too!"' Rhona Le Page's mother went purple in the face when the Salvation Army started speaking to her in French. In her book *The Long Goodbye,* Olive Quinn described her arrival at an evacuee reception centre in Burnley, where the ladies of the WRVS:

> Made signs for us to start eating. We thought this rather odd and would have had a jolly good laugh at their miming had we not been so tired . . . Suddenly the penny dropped, as they say; they thought we were all French and as they could not speak French they had performed this sign language. They were very relieved when they learned we could all speak English!

However, it was the evacuees themselves who sometimes needed the services of a translator, as they encountered the local accents and dialects. During Raymond Carre's first evening in Manchester, an air raid took place and he found himself in a shelter, 'with over a hundred people, young and old, all crowded into that shelter and all talking a broad Lancashire dialect that we could not understand.'

Like many others, Kathleen Cowling soon came to understand 'the Lancashire accent and the different words that people used. Sweets were "toffees", streams were "brooks" and dishes were "pots"!' John Tippett recalls his mother saying:

> I went into the shops and the woman said 'You look starved, love!' I said to her 'I am fine, I have eaten!' The shop woman then explained that, in Stockport, 'starved' meant 'cold'.

Gertrude Brehaut found it very odd that 'people kept calling us "love". We thought it very forward at first, until we realised it was just the way, up north.'

In July 1940 the evacuees began to move out of the reception centres into more permanent accommodation. At this point, hundreds of mothers were scattered throughout England and Scotland, many with babies or infants, with no money or possessions. In the confusion at Weymouth, some had lost what little luggage they had, and a list of the lost items discovered there was displayed for months in Stockport and Bury shop windows. In addition, because Guernsey was occupied by Germany, it was impossible for the evacuees to access the money in their Guernsey bank accounts. Marie Martel recalls:

> Dad could not obtain any money from his bank account. This necessitated him visiting the town hall to ask the mayor for monetary assistance to enable them both to join us in Nuneaton. This must have been so demeaning for him being such an independent man.

Like many other evacuees, Dorothy Cope waited four months for her Guernsey savings to be transferred to the local branch of her bank. By December 1940, Barclays Bank confirmed that it had transferred all of the evacuees' bank balances from Guernsey to local branches in England.[6]

Because of the hasty arrangements surrounding the evacuation, it was difficult for family members to find each other in Britain. Hundreds of mothers spent weeks trying to find children who had been evacuated with their schools, but local councils and newspapers did their best to help. Marlene Whittaker had been evacuated to England with her school, and sent to Glasgow. In the meantime, Marlene's parents, who were English-born, had left Guernsey on a cattle boat with their two other daughters.

> They arrived in Yorkshire, expecting to see me there, and were very upset. My father put an advert in the district newspaper for 'Missing Child'.

Luckily a local saw it and helped to trace Marlene in Glasgow. Soon after, Marlene boarded a train:

> I watched as Glasgow faded in the distance. We arrived at a little railway station in Yorkshire and there was my Dad. I remember grabbing his hand for dear life.

When Mrs Edmonds tried to find members of her family, Wigan Council advised her to contact Nantwich Council where the evacuee school had been transferred to. In Stockport, five-year-old Stanley Bienvenu was seriously ill with bronchial pneumonia and it was not known whether his mother was in England or not. The press launched a nationwide appeal to find Mrs Bienvenu. She was found in Southampton and reunited with her son. The *Stockport Advertiser* later reported:

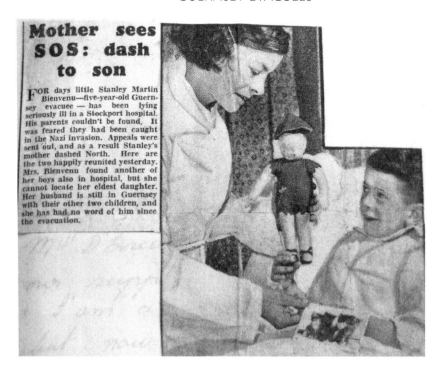

Mother sees SOS: dash to son

FOR days little Stanley Martin Bienvenu—five-year-old Guernsey evacuee — has been lying seriously ill in a Stockport hospital. His parents couldn't be found. It was feared they had been caught in the Nazi invasion. Appeals were sent out, and as a result Stanley's mother dashed North. Here are the two happily reunited yesterday. Mrs. Bienvenu found another of her boys also in hospital, but she cannot locate her eldest daughter. Her husband is still in Guernsey with their other two children, and she has had no word of him since the evacuation.

Stanley Bienvenu press report.

She reached Stockport on Friday evening and a jovial, if not altogether tearless reunion, took place between mother and sick child in his little cubicle. Mrs Bienvenu has five children and they are all with her in Stockport. Her only anxiety now is for her husband's safety. He stayed on in Guernsey and she has only had one wire from him since she left.

John Tippett was evacuated with his school to Shawlands Cross Church, Glasgow where he was looked after by the caretakers, Mr and Mrs Robinson. John's mother sailed to England separately, and arrived in Stockport. After a few weeks she discovered John's whereabouts, and he was escorted by train to Stockport. He walked into the town hall and was horrified by the scene that met his eyes:

The noise and the smell, all the camp beds lined up, people's belongings all over the floor! According to my mum, I didn't take my coat and gas mask off. She said to me 'Take your coat off' and I kept saying to her, 'No, I am going hame' – she was fascinated by my Scots-Guernsey accent! I thought that I was just visiting Mum for the day, and that I was going back to Mrs Robinson in Glasgow.

One Guernsey mother eventually discovered that her daughter had been placed with a Glasgow family, and was reunited with her in Lancashire a few days later. However, her daughter's appearance caused her mother to write to the local billeting officer to complain about the care she had been given:

> I opened her suitcase and found she had so little clothing, she had only a few items and no sleeping garments whatsoever. The socks she had on needed darning, and her summer frock was filthy dirty. I was disgusted! But what annoyed me most – half of her clothing coupons had been used and not a single thing to show for them!

Lawrie Ozanne and his sister Renee decided to take matters into their own hands in order to reunite their family. They sent their new address to the fruit merchant in Halifax to whom their father sold his tomato crops. Mrs Ozanne did the same thing when she arrived in England. When Lawrie's father reached England, he went to Halifax to collect monies owing to him, and was delighted to receive the addresses of all his family members.

The constant movement of Guernsey evacuees around the country during those first months of 1940 is reflected in an evacuee registration list from Stockport Sunday School. It is marked throughout with numerous notes such as 'Transferred to Halifax', 'Transferred to Bowden', indicating that family members had been traced and reunited.

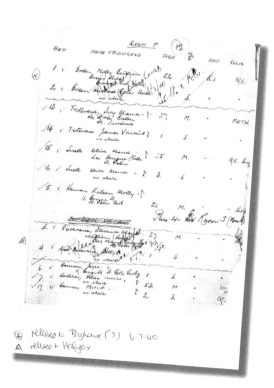

Evacuee registration list.

In some cases, when mothers and children were reunited, they were 'fostered' by local families until they could find their own accommodation. Mavis Brown and her mother were chosen by a Stockport woman:

> We were chosen by a lady who had a child the same age as me, she asked for a lady with a little girl who had dark hair and we 'fitted the bill'. She was very kind, my mother was extremely embarrassed about the fleas and lice that we had caught from the reception centre, and she helped to sort us out. We stayed with her for 3 happy months in all.

Sheila Da Costa was eight years old when her family provided a home for Mrs Hafner and her two children, Nell and Ted, in Eccles:

> I remember the excitement of being told about the evacuation of Guernsey and that we would be taking in a family to give them a temporary home. We enjoyed having them with us and made them very welcome.

Mr and Mrs Langlois and their young son, Robert, were invited into the home of Mr and Mrs Wells, and Mrs Langlois recalled:

Mrs Wells with Robert Langlois.

She went on working in the ATS, and her own husband Victor worked on the railway. As Robert was very poorly we decided it was a godsend, hence we left the school and took our abode with them in quite a nice district.

However, for some mothers, finding somewhere to live was not a happy experience. Many local families were happy to provide a home for one evacuee child, but not enough came forward to take in evacuated mothers with their children. The *Rochdale Observer* observed, 'In the case of unaccompanied children, the securing of homes was quite easy, but the accommodating of mothers and children presented great difficulties and in the final stages, compulsory powers had to be exercised.'

Sheila Brown recalls, 'If anyone came to choose me, my mum came forward and said she was with me, but they didn't want an adult with three boys and a girl as well . . . later the Red Cross found us all an unfurnished house.'

Jean Le Prevost could not find lodgings for herself and her two girls:

At the reception centre, women would try to take one of my girls to live with them, and I would say that we wanted to stay together. Some women actually said to me 'Sorry love, but I don't have room for you and two kiddies.' One whispered 'My husband wouldn't tolerate two women in our house, he thinks that one is enough as it is! In the end I had to let my kiddies go to two separate families until I found an empty flat for us all.

Dulcie Couch arrived in Cheshire with her mother, father and sister:

Whilst my parents tried to find jobs and accommodation, me and my sister were billeted out. After four months my dad got a job on the tugboats and mum became a tram conductress and the family moved into a small flat at Christmas.

Marie Martel, her mother, sister and brother, were eventually housed with Mrs Brown and Marie recalls:

She reluctantly allowed us to stay but here was an elderly lady used to living on her own, now having to share her home with complete strangers . . . in addition because I was twelve years old, I was expected to help her with the housework.

Margaret Cornick and her mother were luckier – 'My mother was fortunate to be hired to be the cook in our Guernsey school, Hollymount Convent, I used to love going up to the kitchen, I used to help sometimes and was able to have a visit with my mum.'

In late July, the *Manchester Guardian* announced that a number of unfurnished houses were ready for the Guernsey adults who had arrived with their children, and the paper appealed to the public for donations of furniture, crockery and household goods, pointing out that, 'it is impossible for the evacuees to move into the houses properly, as they had left their own homes without belongings or money.'

The *Stockport Express* announced:

These evacuees have only beds, a few chairs and an occasional teapot . . . readers of the *Express* probably possess furniture and household utensils for which they have no further need but which would be a God send to evacuees who have been unfortunate enough to lose all their goods and chattels.

Surviving records in local archives and newspapers show that there was a huge response to these newspaper appeals, mostly from working class people who had very little themselves. Girl Guide groups also helped, and in Stockport, Kathleen Potts and her mother knocked on doors, requesting donations of furniture for the evacuees:

People were so generous! They gave us beds, pillows, pillow cases and blankets. We got something from practically every house that we called upon. An announcement was also made at my school that the evacuees needed clothes and people began to give clothes to the school.

An Altrincham newspaper appealed for:

Boots and clothing for 90 boys now billeted in Hale. These boys are in our midst through no fault of their own. They are separated from their parents, their home and their friends, some perhaps never to reunite. Gifts in cash or kind will be gratefully received.

Files in Bury Archives contain details of the numerous household items which were donated by local residents. Mrs Lawrence offered a couch and some chairs, while Mr Charles Parker sent the Guernsey orphan children 49 pairs of slippers and sandals. Letters were sent to many members of Stockport Sunday School's congregation to express, 'Thanks and appreciation to all those who had contributed by gifts of service and goods to help relieve the distress and anxiety which had fallen upon our guests.'

Eva Le Page remembers, 'I left Guernsey with my baby and only a pound note in my purse . . . the Bolton people were very kind and if they helped you, they did it with good hearts. My neighbour was a doctor who lived next door and he helped me a great deal.'

Agnes Scott moved into a house in Manchester:

Word must have got around, for neighbours knocked at the door with all kinds of household equipment which were most useful, as we had nothing. A coal man came with two bags of coal 'With compliments from Mr and Mrs Milligan' – they were an elderly couple, who lived across the road. I will never forget the so many kindnesses we received.

Yvonne Russell's family were offered a tiny house in Halifax, 'at the top of the cellar steps was an old stone trough with one cold tap. That was the kitchen.' Yet the family met with great generosity, and Yvonne wrote:

We would come home to find all sorts of things had been left in the house for us – beds, mattresses, sheets, blankets, crockery, saucepans, cutlery, furniture, even rationed foods. Anything and everything was left for us to find, from packets of tea to bottles of sauce. Some people left notes, so we were able to thank them, but a lot of things just appeared. Fairies were at play in that house. We were so lucky and very amazed at the kindness of the Yorkshire people.

When the Alexandre family moved into an unfurnished house in Edgeley, their daughter Anne remembers, 'The lady next door said "Would you like a chair?" So we said "Oh yes please," and she passed it over, a beautiful little Victorian chair. Then somebody else gave us a rocking chair.'
Edna Cave arrived in Halifax where a neighbour was kindness itself:

Mrs Sykes went round to the neighbours asking if they had any spare bedclothes, and collected crockery, etc. She was so good to me. In the middle of the road there was a coal cellar hole, and the neighbours all clubbed together to buy me half a hundredweight of coal.

Jane Le Page wrote at the time:

People, particularly these Northern women, are very sympathetic. They say things like 'We're all on the same side love, what bits do you need for your house? We will see what we can give you. It's terrible, you, a woman here on her own with three kids and your poor husband stuck at home with them bloody Nazis!

Billeting officers were heavily involved in the lives of the evacuees, and records in Bury Archives show that Tottington's billeting officer, Miss Roberts, was particularly helpful to the Guernsey mothers. Guernsey man Sergeant Aylward

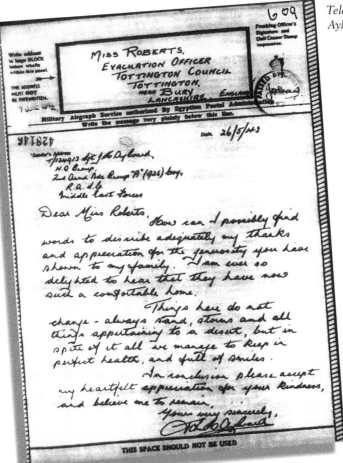

Telegram from Sergeant Aylward.

was serving in the Middle East and sent a telegram to Miss Roberts, expressing his thanks, 'How can I possibly find words to describe adequately my thanks and appreciation for the generosity you have shown to my family. I am so delighted to hear that they have now such a comfortable home.'

However, Joan Simon recalls that her billeting officer put pressure on her to place her children permanently with a local family:

He told me that we women could not possibly cope without our husbands, who were of course either trapped in Guernsey or fighting in the British forces. I felt sure that I could somehow manage to look after my own children! And they were all that I had left.

Others encountered problems when they attempted to rent flats and houses. They were advised that, unless their husbands were fighting in the forces, they could not rent property. To overcome this problem, mothers whose husbands were in the forces teamed up with mothers whose husbands were trapped in occupied Guernsey. In numerous cases, two or more Guernsey mothers shared empty properties with their respective children during the war. They shared financial control of the household as well as childcare responsibilities. Many could not manage on the public assistance allowance that they received, and undertook part-time work. John Tippet recalls:

> My mum, my granny and Aunt Cissy Le Poidevin shared an empty corner shop as my dad was fighting in North Africa and Cissy's husband was in Guernsey. They took turns to run the house, look after us children and they also worked in the same cinema but on different shifts.

Anne Le Noury has distinct memories of officials checking the activities of the adult evacuees because anyone receiving public assistance was not supposed to take up employment. She recalls, 'Mum lived in dread of being in trouble with the authorities and feared that her children might be taken away from her.' However, in some cases the strain of sharing accommodation led to friction. Four Guernsey mothers and their children were crammed into a house which became known as 'The Guernsey Hostel', and Rose Short recalls:

Mrs Le Noury.

Each mother and her children had one bedroom in the house, and they lived communally with my mum as the leader. There was also a woman 'overseer' who I think was from the WVS. This constant interference from the overseer didn't work very well as you can imagine, and there were arguments sometimes between the mothers, I think mainly over cooking and childcare.

This was not an isolated case, and wartime records describe the cramped conditions in a house in Wakefield which had been designed for one family, but was being shared by four Channel Island mothers and their respective children. During wartime, empty properties that were in good condition were often requisitioned by the forces, so several Guernsey families were offered accommodation that was practically unfit for human habitation. Ida Donaldson arrived in England with a ten-week-old baby and two small children. They moved into a house in Stockport that was, 'a bit of a shack . . . the house next door was bombed in an air raid and we were told that our house was not safe.' Rhona Le Page's family was offered a house in Burnley which was 'not fit for pigs to live in!' Eva Le Page moved into a flat and during the first night she discovered insects creeping along the walls, 'we slept on the floor with the candles lit, and I had to move out at once.' Edna Cave moved into a room, and the next morning:

> I woke up and there were bugs on the wall, I didn't have much but I was clean! I had a match box and put two or three of the bugs into the match box to show the council that I was telling the truth. I said 'I am not going back there!'

Ruth Alexandre spent a whole day viewing dilapidated houses in Rawtenstall, and wrote in her diary 'we can have a choice of Victor Place or Swinshaw Cottage. After visiting them both, I thought, I may be a refugee, but I have some pride!' Mrs Le Noury was offered a house that had been condemned just before the war, and her daughter Anne described it thus:

> Our neighbours included jailbirds and prostitutes . . . once entry was gained into our cellar, it was only a few steps up to a cellar door. One push would force the small bolt and our few possessions were there for the taking. Once my mother discovered who'd taken our few toys and Christmas gifts – she went to the house, but refused to take them back . . . she'd found everything in a dirty, flea-infested house where the children slept with the dogs.

Anne Mauger described the conditions in the house that she and her parents shared:

There was water running down the walls and the house was full of cockroaches. During air-raids my parents had to stand in the cellar, knee deep in cold water, passing me back and forward between them.

Several Guernsey women were made to 'earn their keep' despite the fact that their billeter received an allowance to cover the cost of feeding them. Before they obtained their own house, Mrs Le Noury and her children were billeted with a Stockport couple who worked at a munitions factory at night, and Anne Le Noury recalls:

They slept during the day so we were told not to make any noise, also Mum was expected to look after their boy. She said that she was treated as a household drudge. Mum sought refuge by going to the park as often as possible.

Dorothy Johnson was selected by a well-spoken lady:

She looked me up and down and said 'Can you cook?' 'Yes I can,' I replied. She said 'Right, you look strong enough, you will do.' I moved in with the couple in a Rectory and became their housekeeper for six months. I was given ten shillings and board and lodging. I worked very hard indeed and never received a smile from either of them. He would come home at all hours and I was expected to get out of bed and cook a meal for him, no matter what time it was. He would then get up early the next day and I was expected to do the same. After six months of this, my husband, Henry, left the forces as he had failed a medical. He was allowed to move into the Rectory but my wages were docked to cover his board and lodgings. Eventually we managed to get our own home.

In July 1940 people began to visit the evacuee reception centres to choose a Guernsey schoolchild to take home, taking on the role of 'foster parent'. They could not have foreseen that many of them would have responsibility for that child for five years! Each child's experience of being chosen is very different, but some are included here. Jeffrey Le Page recalls:

It was the little girls that seemed to be chosen first, and it soon became evident that the hall was rapidly emptying of girls, leaving just the boys behind. My sister was picked very quickly and when we saw each other, once a week, she would tell me about always helping around the house. I never did any of that!

In Oldham, nine-year-old John Bougourd and his friend David were not chosen by any of the families:

All the little children disappeared quickly, particularly the little girls, and we were left behind. The two WVS ladies who were in charge actually took David and I home with them and we lived very happily with Mrs Mason for 3 years.

Brian and George Brown heard one couple say, 'If we take those growing lads, they will eat us out of house and home and I just cant afford it.' However, in country areas, farmers viewed growing boys as ideal for carrying out heavy farm work. After spending three weeks in Wigan, John and Alf's Laine's school party was moved to Nantwich in Cheshire. John and Alf were chosen by a farming family from Ridley, and John recalled:

We enjoyed the life at first, helping in various ways, but unfortunately it became very demanding as harvesting began. The School Inspector came to see why we were absent from school and took us back, post haste, and we were re-billeted.

Roy Simon was also chosen by a farmer in Cheshire:

My time spent on that farm is etched in my memory as being very tough and unhappy. Billy and I had to work like Trojans; pigsties, animals, land work, we were like adult farm workers only not too well treated. After a few months I was rescued by my dad who had been walking around the local farms looking for me! He saw the state of me and started berating the farmer and his wife. They said that I was billeted with them and I was jolly well going to stay and work on the farm! But Dad produced 'proof of ownership' and I was off!

Sometimes the gender of the child already living in the home influenced the choice of evacuee. Most of the evacuees were fostered by working class families, whose terraced homes had only two bedrooms. It would have been considered 'more decent' for a boy to share a bedroom with another boy, and a girl with another girl. The evacuee billeting allowance was paid directly to the wife, which would have been welcome during a time when many working class wives had no idea how much their husbands actually earned. Marian Marchington's father was on the billeting committee in Disley, and she recalls the day he brought a Guernsey evacuee home:

We were a family of eight, living in a two up, two down terraced house. My father walked in holding the hand of Morris. We had him in our family the whole of the war. He was dressed in a little grey suit of short trousers . . . he just fitted in with us. My mother was very protective of him.

Fred Jones stated:

> Dad read us newspaper reports about the kiddies needing homes. I didn't know where the Islands were and Dad said that they were part of Britain but that on a map they were very close to the French coast. He said 'Maybe we should take one of them, a little boy, so you can play together?' Mum took me with her to the church hall and we saw Joe there. He looked so scared. Mum said 'Would you like that little boy to come and live with us?' I said 'Yes please' – he shared my bedroom with me and was like a brother to me. Mum couldn't have any more children after she had me, and Joe was like her second son.

Ruth Harrison's family chose a little Guernsey girl, Win De La Mare, to stay with them, and Ruth recalls, 'Mum said she had chosen a little girl so she could come and play with me like a sister, and Win did become like my own sister. We are still constantly in touch.'

Jennifer Rose's family took in two female evacuees, a Manchester evacuee and a Guernsey girl, and Jennifer recalls:

> We looked after Rachel from Manchester for about eight months. We got on really well with her but she got letters from her mum and dad, and her mum came to visit her several times by bus. But when Joan arrived from Guernsey, her mum was left behind, so Joan never got anything from her family. We really took her into our hearts and are still in touch. This was a very different experience to having Rachel.

Dulcie and Yvonne Ogier were cared for by the Fisher family in Nantwich, who treated them like their own children. At one time the Fishers enquired about adoption, but Mr Ogier refused to allow this. George Clarke was nine when he was chosen by a couple in Lymm, Cheshire, whose son was seventeen years old – 'They took me home, saying "You will be good friends with our own son, but he is a bit bigger than you." We did become good friends, but he was called up into the army a year later.'

Mrs Davis had planned to take home one girl as a companion for her daughter Dorothy, who remembers:

> Two girls stood very close together, as if daring anyone to separate them. They had this look in their eyes, full of appeal and longing to be chosen. I went completely overboard and prevailed upon my mum to take both girls. 'It will be alright, I will manage!' I said. And so began our extended family with Elaine and Olive, and the loving friendship which still thrives today.[7]

Dulcie and Yvonne Ogier with Mrs Fisher.

Len Robilliard was chosen by Mr and Mrs Smith, while his brother and sister lived with families on the same road, 'all three of us were extremely lucky to be accepted in good homes.' Ron Gould and Graham Froome were chosen by Miss Yearsley and her father:

Miss Yearsley was very kind and showed a lot of interest in us and our families. Both Graham and I only had a change of underwear and a spare shirt and jacket or blazer and a pair of short trousers. Miss Yearsley took us both into Lewis's, the big store in Manchester, and fitted us both up with a new grey suit each. I am sure they paid for this themselves.

Kathleen Cowling was initially housed with her school in Rochdale, but later the pupils were told that they were to live with local families. Kathleen recalls:

I was only told the night before where I was going to go and it was with a few tears that I packed my few belongings into a battered suitcase which I still have. I believe that some Guernsey evacuees were publicly 'chosen' by their hosts, a very upsetting procedure. We were more fortunate and I was taken to a lady who lived on her own and wanted female company. My new auntie looked after me for three years.

Ron and Graham in their new suits.

Mavis de la Mare recalled her arrival in Disley:

> We were taken to St Mary's School where local people came to choose a
> Guernsey child. It was very overwhelming the day I was introduced to my
> foster parents. They had no children of their own but they welcomed me into
> their home and I spent five happy years with them.[8]

A handful of the evacuees interviewed for this book were fostered by families
that were a little wealthier. George Gallienne was fostered by a caring widow
in Alderley Edge, Mrs Bell. 'I have fond memories of frequent holidays in
Llandudno. Christmas 1940 was particularly special for a ten-year-old. I had a
Hornby train set from Father Christmas.'

The Bowditch family were offered the Lodge on Lady Reynolds' estate in
Heaton Mersey, Stockport, which enabled the five family members to remain
together throughout the war. Mary Bowditch recalls, 'after the war, Lady
Reynolds continued to send us birthday and Christmas cards.' Joan Cheshire
arrived in Stockport and was separated from her mother and sister. She was
chosen by a Mr and Mrs Pickstock who 'had a really huge house, I had my own
bedroom and bathroom and they bought me new clothes.'

For six months, Dorothy Ogier found herself living with the Thornton family
in Glasgow, who gave her the finest of food, clothes, toys and books. Eventually,
Dorothy's mother located her, and Dorothy was put on a train to Manchester.
As she waited on the railway platform, she spotted her family:

My heart sank as I looked at this scruffy woman with her grubby kids. I wanted to go straight back to Mrs Thornton, who was clean and respectable with nice clothes and a gentle voice . . . it started to sink in, we are still poor and this is real life, and life in Glasgow was like a dream, just pretend.

However, not all the evacuees were totally happy in these upper class homes. Frank Le Poidevin was the headmaster of Torteval School, and took his family and pupils to England, where they eventually settled in the prosperous village of Alderley Edge, Cheshire. Frank's family was billeted with one of the wealthiest families in the village, and his son, Nick, recalls:

We found ourselves dwellers in a no-man's land, in an invidious 'between stairs' position . . . we were given a bedroom on the same level as the family, but we were considered below them in social status. We were to use the

Torteval evacuees at Alderley Edge (above) and a Torteval School label (right).

servants' staircase that led past the kitchen and the servants' wing, but we were considered too highly placed to be welcome there.

Walter Robilliard was evacuated to the same village, where he played with his foster parents' middle class children and the local working class children, but noticed that his foster parents' children never played with the working class children.
Although the majority of the child evacuees interviewed for this book were well cared for by their foster parents, several others experienced forms of abuse, but not all wish to go on public record. Mary was evacuated at an early age and fostered by a Lancashire couple:

> When the mother was out at work, her husband often sat me on his lap and showed me strange books. I later realised they were books about gynaecology. At the time I didn't understand the books but I knew that something was not right.

One boy, Maurice, was billeted with the Clarke family and made to care for their bedridden grandmother, often missing school in the process. He was also made to eat his meals off newspaper on the floor. His sister Joan was billeted with a different family in the same area, and when she visited her brother, she noticed how unhappy he was with the Clarkes. She told one of the nuns at their Guernsey Catholic school, then tried to see her brother again. Mrs Clarke told Joan to 'go and see the billeting officer', and slammed the door in her face. After some time, it was discovered that Maurice had been moved to a remand home miles away, and Joan recalls:

> The Manager had been told by the billeting officer that Maurice was a difficult child to place and that he had no living relatives! It took us a few weeks to get him out of there – we told the nuns at our school who told the local priest, who appealed to the bishop!

Financial gain sometimes played its part in the fostering of evacuees, and Rosemary Hall and her brother suffered in a Birkenhead billet:

> My brother and I stood in a church hall for ages, people wanted me but not my brother. A woman said 'I will have the little girl' but she was told 'They don't want to be separated.' The woman said 'I don't want two of them.' The Salvation Army said 'if you take them both you will get nearly 20s a week to keep them.' The woman quickly changed her mind. We spent a horrendous four months sleeping on camp beds in her hallway behind the front door. We weren't allowed in any other part of the house except the hall and the lavatory

in the back yard, we were constantly hungry. She clearly took us in to get the regular twenty shillings. After four months, our mum tracked us down. She knocked on the door of the house, saw the state of us, and removed us immediately from the premises without waiting for the woman to come back from the shops. She took us into a little flat that she had found in Bury. We were much happier there.

Ruth Harrison recalled an unpleasant incident at an evacuee reception centre:

My mum was about to choose a Guernsey evacuee girl to take home with her, and was told by a rather posh WRVS lady, 'Don't worry dear, we will find you a decent one!' My mum was appalled and I will never forget her reply – 'They are not commodities, Madam, they are children!'

During the Second World War, the separation of children from their parents was viewed more casually than it is today. John Welshman has studied wartime evacuation at length and believes that evacuation would not happen today 'because changes in the way that child abuse has been exposed mean that children would never be sent away to live with strangers.'[9]

NOTES

1   Island Archive, Guernsey, Muriel Parsons Diary, June 1940. 'It Happened to Me', p. 24.
2   Bury Archives, ABU/2/3/11/6, Channel Islands Correspondence File.
3   Notes for Billeting Officers and Voluntary Welfare Workers, (Ministry of Health: London, 1939), p. 14.
4   Lewis family papers, *Guernsey Star*, undated but printed between 20 June and the occupation of 30 June 1940; the newspaper was controlled by German authorities during the occupation.
5   *Horsforth at War*, Saville Creative Communications, Leeds, 2005.
6   Barclays Bank Archive, Letter from Barclays Bank London to Southampton branch, 10 December 1940.
7   Memories of Dorothy Davies, *Guernsey Press Supplement*, June 2000, p. 15.
8   Thompson family archive, 'Carrie's War' programme, GADOC.
9   John Welshman, *Churchill's Children: The Evacuation Experience in Wartime Britain*, (OUP: Oxford, 2010), p. 80.

3

SETTLING INTO THE COMMUNITY

It took little time for most of them who could take up employment
to become self-supporting members of our community, with
considerable determination to help in our war effort.[1]

The Guernsey evacuees integrated into their new communities, standing
alongside local people when doing vital war work, and huddling in
shelters with them during the bombing raids. Thousands 'did their bit' for
Britain, including men, women and children, and one Channel Islander noted:

A large number of Channel Islanders are holding high office in the Church,
Judiciary, Navy, Army, Air Force and Civil Service, as well as those who have
attained eminence in medicine, education and other great professions, and we
are proud of the satisfaction being given by our workmen in unfamiliar jobs
throughout the length and breadth of this land.

Thousands of evacuees joined the forces or the Home Guard, became fire
watchers, and contributed towards local war effort campaigns. One Guernsey
woman wrote to the *Sunday Express*, stating:

I have lost in this war many things that were dear to me. A cosy little home in
Guernsey, now occupied by jackbooted ruffians . . . the companionship of a
young husband who dreams his dreams behind barbed wire in Germany. We
are behind you to a woman.

Winifred Best found work at the Wellington bomber factory in Blackpool, and when she was seventeen and a half, she and her friend went to join the Women's Auxiliary Air Force. They intended to do clerical work but discovered that the only openings were for flight mechanics:

> We said, 'Well we will have a go!' and I understand that we were only the second group of women ever to do so. We were both posted to Hednesford where we had female drill sergeants, and six of us trained for 6 months – one girl was from Jersey. We mixed with the men, they saw us a bit of a joke, six women among all these men.

Winifred was invalided out of the force in early 1944, and returned to Blackpool where she obtained a clerical post in the Treasury Finance Department at the County Hotel:

Winifred Le Page (centre) in the WAAF.

In February 1944 they put me in a job relating to Operation Overlord, what we now call D-Day. I kept accounts of all the ports in the south of England that were building up stocks of oil and coal for D-Day, and how much fuel our ships were taking on abroad. I was locked in my office all day as it was so top secret and I had to make a phone call if I wanted to go to the toilet! After D-Day we didn't have to be locked in any more!

During the war, at least five Channel Islanders were members of the Manchester Auxiliary Fire Brigade, coping with devastating destruction, particularly during the Manchester Blitz of December 1940. Ron Le Moignan's father joined the brigade, as did Betty Warr's father, Harry Ross. Lawson Allez worked as a lorry driver during the day, but he and his brother worked with the brigade at night. Raymond Carre joined the Halifax Fire Service and during a training course near Hull, he had a terrifying experience:

The city was in flames, bombs were falling all around us as we approached. Suddenly a large bomb landed just ahead of us, the crew were scattered. I wandered around for what seemed like an eternity . . . I had lost my steel helmet, the straps had broken, my glasses had gone and it was dark. There was fire and smoke everywhere. I was alone. I eventually arrived at the fire station's meeting point where the fire officer greeted me with the words 'Where have you been Fireman Carre? Your steel helmet was found badly buckled, straps gone and only identifiable by your number 394999.' Truly an emergency number!

Men and women from a small rural island found themselves working in large factories making ammunition, aircraft, army uniforms and parachutes. Muriel Bougourd's father was over the age limit that the forces required, 'he was put to war work immediately, and worked in munitions and aircraft factories all through the war.' Robert Langlois' father, Dudley, worked in engineering, then for the RAF recovering crashed aircraft, then joined the forces in June 1943. Len Robilliard worked in a factory which made engines for warships and landing craft, and silent pumps for submarines. Paul Blicq made parts for Lancaster bombers, while his brother Phil undertook fire watching. In Bury, Daphne Guille and her sister made webbing for army kit bags and uniforms:

The girls that we worked with in the factory were very kind to us. They brought us things such as pillows, bedding and some dresses too, they knew we had arrived with nothing. Later we went to work in munitions at Ferrantis.

At the age of fourteen, Ron Gould began work at R.J. Patchett's in Bradford, which manufactured handles and corner pieces for ammunition boxes:

Raymond Carre and the Halifax Fire Service band.

Manchester Auxiliary Fire Brigade.

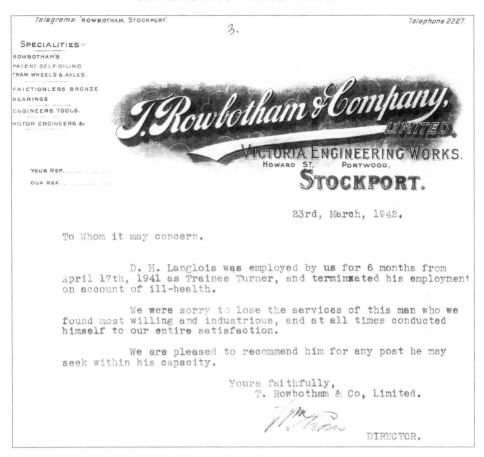

Job reference for Mr D. Langlois.

the Carpenters in the woodshop were very good to me during my first winter at work. They very kindly made me a lovely sledge . . . everyone was always so kind to me.

Agnes Scott remembers her first week at a factory in Northenden:

I had to work a week in hand before getting paid, and had no money so walked to and from work. The foreman, John Dewhurst, noticed that I never went to the canteen and wanted to know the reason. He gave me a loan of 10s. I was delighted – it was so unexpected. I never forgot him.

Marie Martel's father found work at a car factory which was now making ammunition, 'and he nearly caused a strike by not claiming for 20 minutes' overtime he'd worked!' Peter Ninnim's father was a master carpenter and tried to join the RAF but was told that his was a reserved occupation.

Spitfire Fund ribbon.

He found work in Hazel Grove making wings and tails for Mosquito aircraft and was also an ARP Warden. Adolphus Ogier found work at a Stockport factory but quickly changed his name to 'Bill' due to the hatred of the name 'Adolf' in England during the war. Child evacuees did their bit too, collecting salvage, packing Red Cross parcels, and helping to raise money for the local 'Spitfire Funds'. The Elizabeth College boys joined the Officers Training Corps and the Home Guard. Working alongside local people in this way gave the evacuees a clear sense that they were part of the war machine, helping Britain in the fight against Germany.

In common with their neighbours, many evacuees endured the terror of air raids, and some did not live to see Guernsey again. Marie and Mona Martel recall:

We had a small brick air-raid shelter at the bottom of the garden which we shared with our neighbours Mrs Wright and her children Danny and Eileen, her husband being in the RAF. This was used mostly during night raids, when we would take our blankets with us.

Margaret Carberry remember bombs falling around her school premises:

We often had air raids and we had to all get out of bed and go over to another building which had a basement. One night there was a raid and we weren't in that building, it must have been an act of God because that building was badly damaged, some of us could have been killed or injured that night . . . we found pieces of shrapnel and kept these for souvenirs.

John Davis recalls an evening when the some of the Elizabeth College boys were sleeping in an aircraft hangar:

A stray German bomber, having failed to drop all of its load on Manchester, dropped two bombs, one either side of the hangar. The blast blew the windows in and us out of our camp beds. Our teacher, Jack Reddish called out 'Half a crown to the first boy who can reach the far corner of the airfield and get back to me!' This was five weeks' pocket money so we were all off! It was an excellent piece of quick thinking for, by the time we returned, any form of shock had been completely forgotten.

Judith Glanville recalled, 'I had only been at the school for two weeks when a bomb was dropped on the hockey pitch and we were showered with glass in the dining room.' Muriel Bougourd used to hide under the kitchen table during air raids, 'for many years into adulthood I could never get up at night or early morning without shaking.' There were no full bombing raids on Blackpool, but Winifred Le Page recalled:

We could see the flames and smoke as they bombed Liverpool, then the British fighters used to chase the German planes from Liverpool and they came over Blackpool, and the Germans often decided to get rid of their bombs and dropped them anywhere.

Anne Alexandre's family were evacuated to Stockport but moved to Coventry because there was plenty of work there, and they were assured it was 'safe as houses'. Five months later, Anne and her brother were walking along the street when a German aircraft appeared overhead, and began to machine gun the street, 'I could see the stones flying out of the wall and all the bullets . . . he was so low that I could see him grinning.' A few days later the Coventry Blitz began in earnest, and Anne's family were in their home when another raid began, 'all these bombs were coming down thicker and faster, that was the worst night of the Coventry Blitz. Suddenly there was a very close bomb and the conservatory doors blew in.' The family moved from Coventry, and eventually ended up back in Stockport where Anne's father, Jim, joined the Essential Works Department, building airfields.

At the age of thirteen, Peter Rouxel was caught up in an air raid, 'I was not hurt physically but my nerves went to pieces, and I spent three months recovering in a military hospital in Macclesfield.' Cathy and Pamela Hammond's family suffered a great loss during an air raid in Bolton:

One of the air raid wardens came to help my mother by carrying my baby brother whilst she looked after Pamela and me. Unknown to my mother, he dropped my brother on the way to the shelter. On arrival, he handed him back and did not say what had happened. Nicholas died during the night, leaving my mother shocked and devastated. She later learned that the warden had been too afraid to say anything.

John Laine was living in Oldham with Mr and Mrs Hughes, their son John and daughter Ida, where he shared a bedroom with John Hughes. At midnight on 12 October 1941, the air raid sounded, as it had done so many times before:

> But almost immediately we heard a bomb screaming down. John and I were still in bed, despite having been called some seconds before to get up and dress. This was the last I knew for some time . . . on coming to, [I] found myself buried under the debris. We had gone through the floor and I could feel the bricks, heavy masonry and flagstones from the pavement on top of me and smell the gas from the shattered mains. I can recollect very vividly praying earnestly as I waited for help . . . a fireman came and dug me out . . . I was able to tell them that John was buried too. I learned later that he had been killed, and minutes later his mother also died.

In 1942, Florence Le Tissier was being treated in hospital, and the patients were told that, in the event of an air raid warning, they were to hide underneath their beds. Florence was too weak to leave her bed, so was ordered to remain there during air raids. However, one day the siren sounded, and a nearby patient panicked and screamed at Florence to get under her bed. As Florence struggled to get out of bed, she hit her head on the floor, which caused a blood clot on the brain and subsequently killed her.

Although most evacuees integrated into the community, they also remained in close contact with other evacuees in the area, to replace the friends and family that they had left behind in Guernsey. They realised that one day they would return home, and would need to pick up the pieces of their pre-war lives. In order that the staff and pupils of the evacuated schools could remain together during the war, a number of Guernsey headteachers re-established their schools in England. The story of one of these Guernsey schools will be discussed in detail in chapter five.

In July 1940, leading Channel Islanders in London formed the 'Channel Islands Refugee Committee' (CIRC) which became the centre of the evacuee community in Britain. On 6 July 1940 the CIRC issued a press release in *The Times* to describe its aims, and the BBC immediately broadcast the story. Within hours there was a queue of evacuees outside the CIRC office, asking for help, and letters arrived every day asking for aid. The press and radio announcements clearly touched the hearts of the British public, as sacks full of letters and donations poured into the CIRC office. The CIRC had no idea that the response from the public would be so overwhelming, and by the end of 1940 they had received over £24,000 in donations.

They created three separate departments to meet the needs of their evacuees – Clothing, Relief and Records. The Relief department offered help to the most vulnerable evacuees, the unaccompanied schoolchildren and the mothers with infants. Cash payments were provided as well as grants for equipment. When Mrs Lenfestey made a request for a sewing machine grant, Guernsey headmaster Percy Martel wrote a letter of support for her:

> A sewing machine would help her to gain more income for her children and herself, she could alter her children's clothes when necessary, and she could also alter other Evacuees' clothes as and when. She is a good mother whose husband was left behind on Guernsey, and she is doing all that she can for her family on a small amount of public assistance.

As Christmas 1940 approached, the CIRC, who were evacuees themselves, knew there would be little money available for festive food or presents for evacuees separated from their families through war. They advised the Guernsey teachers:

> You will be pleased to hear that this committee is able to give a Christmas present of one shilling to every unaccompanied school child – the committee sends its wishes for a happy Christmas to the children, teachers and helpers.

The Guernsey Forest School used this money to pay for a trip to the cinema, and a Christmas tea party. As demands on the committee's funds increased during the war, the amount sent to the children at Christmas had to be reduced – the 1944 payment to Bury evacuees was 30 per cent lower than that of 1943. Thankfully, wartime newspapers show that many local authorities, and the ladies of the WRVS, provided Christmas tea parties and entertainment for the Guernsey children.

In the late summer of 1940, the CIRC feared that the Ministry of Health would not be able to reclothe every Channel Island child, so they sent memos to Guernsey teachers to obtain details of the clothing and footwear that were required. One stated:

> We were shocked to hear that some of our children were practically barefooted . . . if this is the case, please let us know at once what sum of money you require to remedy the situation.

The CIRC received a bill from Glasgow Council for £2,900 to cover the cost of supplying clothing to Guernsey children, but luckily donations from both the UK and abroad were now flooding into the CIRC offices. In July 1941 the CIRC made the momentous decision not to obtain clothing through the WRVS, but to purchase clothing themselves. An explanation for this decision is provided in chapter five. By October 1941 the CIRC had set up several clothing

Cheshire evacuees' Christmas party.

stores where the evacuees could choose their own clothes, using their clothing coupons. The CIRC also began to receive letters from evacuees who wanted to find relatives from the islands who were believed to be in the UK. A Records department was quickly established to take on this task. Mrs Bretel asked Bury Council for help in tracing her husband, and was told, 'I would suggest that you contact the CIRC at 34 Victoria Street, London, where they have a complete list of evacuees from the Channel Islands.'

The CIRC began to record, not just the details of every evacuee, but also the name of every Islander who was known to have remained behind. By 1944, around 30,000 names and addresses had been gathered.

The 'Guernsey community' was strengthened by the formation of around ninety Channel Island societies. The first was established in Halifax in September 1940, and forty evacuees attended the first meeting, most of whom were from Guernsey. These societies collected membership subscriptions, raised funds and organised regular meetings and social events. Societies in Lancashire and Cheshire organised outings to Belle Vue Pleasure Grounds in Manchester. Many societies established Welfare Committees which worked with the CIRC to obtain grants, legal advice and clothing for their members. At Christmas the societies organised tea parties for the children, often in conjunction with the local council.

Programme for Belle Vue, Manchester.

There was no postal service between Guernsey and England during the war, and the only form of communication was through British Red Cross letters. In November 1940 the evacuees were allowed to send their first messages to Guernsey, their first real contact with home. At first they were only allowed to write ten words, but this later increased to twenty-five. To reach Guernsey, the letters travelled through several European countries and were censored by German administrators. The evacuees did not receive replies to this first batch of letters until March and April 1941, when Ruth Alexandre wrote in her diary, 'What a thrill, the first messages arrived for me from home! Anne came round, also John and Fred to hear about them.' Anne Le Noury explained how important these letters were to evacuees, 'The rare occasion when Mum received a Red Cross letter was like the biggest event ever. The few censored words meant that Dad and the family in Guernsey were still alive.'

Frank Le Messurier sent a letter to his parents asking them if he could join the merchant navy, 'and it took two months for my letter to bring the reply "Yes".' Percy Rowland told his mother that his wife, Muriel, had just given birth to a baby boy, Richard. Pamela le Poidevin sent a Red Cross letter to her father, telling him that on Christmas Day she had been recovering in Stockport Infirmary. Suddenly people around her realised that she was an evacuee who was not going to receive any Christmas presents from home, and Pam recalls 'there was a scramble to find some things for me from Father Christmas.' She also received a visit from the Mayor and Lady Mayoress of Stockport.

Red Cross letters from Guernsey often contained secret codes, such as 'Morris left us', which meant that the Germans had taken away the family car. 'Mother Hubbard has not been' meant that there was enough food available, while another common code was 'See Marc every day' or 'Marc is my best friend' which meant that the writer was secretly listening to the BBC on a Marconi radio, to learn about the real progress of the war. However, some of the letters passed sad news between England and Guernsey in a few stilted words. Daphne Guille told her family that her sister's child had died eleven months earlier, 'Baby Mary Laine died December 1940'. One Guernsey family received a message which simply said that their son had died in England. They had sent two sons to England, so for several months they had no idea which of them was dead. Because birthday and Christmas cards could not be posted between Guernsey to England, the cards sent between the evacuees made up in some way for this loss. Some still survive between the pages of diaries, and were either bought, hand-made, or produced by charities such as the Red Cross. Some evacuees also received Christmas telegrams from Guernsey people who were serving in the forces.

Pam Le Poidevin in hospital.

From :

WAR ORGANISATION OF THE BRITISH RED CROSS AND ORDER OF ST. JOHN

To :

Comité International
de la Croix Rouge
Genève

Foreign Relations
Department.

Expéditeur   SENDER   Absender

Name ...Rowland...................................
Nom
Christian name ......P.G.............................
Vorname Prènom
Address ....RED CROSS MESSAGE...........
Adresse
........................BUREAU 785,..................
.....................WELLINGTON ST,.................
...........................STOCKPORT..................

MESSAGE   Mitteilung
(Not more than 25 words)   (25 mots au maximum)   (Nicht über 25 Worte)

Dear Mum, Muriel has a Baby Boy.//

born early hours August 2nd. Named Richard Mal-

-colm. Both doing fine. Am very excited.

Best love Percy.

Date Datum.......... **3 AUG 1943**

Destinataire   ADDRESSEE   Empfänger

Name ....Rowland.........................
Nom
Christian name ....Mrs A.L.................
Vorname Prènom
Address ....
Adresse
........." Castle View".......................
Les Amballes...............................
St. Johns   Guernsey   C.I.

Reply overleaf (not more than 25 words)
Réponse au verso (25 mots au maximum)
Antwort umseitig (nicht über 25 Worte)

27 AOOT

Red Cross letter from Percy Rowland.

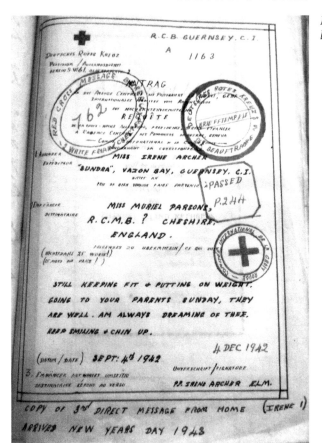

Muriel Parsons' Red Cross letter.

The regular Channel Island Society meetings were very important to the evacuees as they were able to talk with those who understood what they were going through. One Islander wrote:

This society is doing the very important war work of serving as an outpost of our beloved Islands, and a rallying point to which our members can bring their news and their troubles. As comrades bound together, we bear one another's burdens and share one another's joys.

Mrs Lowe shared a house with her children and father-in-law, and noted in her diary:

My father in law is driving me to distraction. Nothing is good enough for him, and I only hold my tongue for the sake of my poor husband who is trapped in Guernsey. Please God we return home soon and my father in law can move back into his own cottage! The Society meetings are my only break from him!

Muriel Parsons' Red Cross Christmas card.

Channel Island Society Christmas card.

Channel Islanders serving in the forces attended meetings whenever they could. Winifred Best and a friend attended a meeting in Wolverhampton, travelling by train and trolley bus from their WAAF camp:

> We had a wonderful time, but when we came home and got on the trolley bus it broke down! Finally they got out another trolley bus for us . . . it was 10 p.m. by the time we got to Walsall and there were no trains until 1–2 a.m., now we were AWOL! There was nothing we could do, we had a meal at a Red Cross forces canteen. We didn't get back to our camp until 3 a.m. and faced a very angry camp guard!

Channel Island societies arranged events such as card games, raffles and dances. Lawrence Torode became Secretary of the Bury Society at the age of seventeen, and recalls numerous tea dances and tea parties. The society even hired the Palais De Dance, attracting evacuees from Bury, Manchester, Bolton, Burnley and Rochdale. The Burnley Society organised cards and ludo for children, and a concert evening every Friday. Mary Le Huray recalled, 'It was great to meet the other kids and run wild for a bit in the church hall. There were always sandwiches and cakes for us, I don't know how they managed to provide them!'

However Clem Brehaut pointed out that, for the adult evacuees, 'these meetings very often ended in tears, not knowing who would meet again, due to air raids and bombings.'

Channel Island Society meeting, Nantwich.

Channel Island Society meeting, Stockport.

Arguably the most influential society was the Stockport and District Channel Island Society, formed in January 1941. Five miles south of Manchester's city centre, the society had around 800 members, 500 of whom were adults. The *Stockport Advertiser* described the first meeting thus:

> 250 evacuees attended, and folk who have long been separated from their homes and friends were eager for news; the most popular speakers were those who were able to give news of home, or of friends who are now scattered up and down the land.

Stockport's committee included Percy Martel, headmaster of Guernsey's Forest School, and Herbert Brelsford. Herbert had brought the St Peter in the Wood School to England and was appointed acting head of Disley School when its headmaster was called into the forces. The committee organised numerous fundraising events, including one at the Ritz cinema which featured Norman Evans, the star of a recent Royal Command Performance. By 1941, the society had raised enough funds to open its own clothing store. Ruth Alexandre was on the committee, and her diary describes visits to evacuees to discover their needs. She often spent the mornings investigating welfare cases, and the afternoons sorting through clothing donations. She visited a home in Bramwell Street, and noted, 'What a job to find the house, I walked miles, and spent an hour there.' On another occasion she wrote, 'my visit was a waste of time as the man has authorisation for new clothes already!'

However, the Stockport society's main achievement was its newsletter, the *Channel Islands Monthly Review*. In May 1941 a four-page news sheet was produced, which by 1944 had grown in size to twenty-four pages. Roger Simon's sister typed the magazine on a manual typewriter which had been donated to the society through an appeal printed in the local paper. Ruth Alexandre wrote, 'I spent the whole day packing the *Review,* ready for posting out to members,' while a month later, she noted, 'for the first time I was allowed to sub-edit the *Review*, with blue pencil!' The magazine was originally produced for Stockport's members only, but other societies began to order copies, and soon each print run was for 5,000 copies. The Gosport Society ordered 36 copies of the magazine in June 1943.

The August 1940 issue of the magazine included an editorial, a letters page, Channel Island songs and poetry, and details of the activities of other societies. The 'enquiries' page contained messages from evacuees who were trying to locate friends and family. There was news of Islanders in the forces, and of those interned in German camps. A section was devoted to the most important content, the Red Cross messages recently received from the Channel Islands. The fact that these often intimate messages were printed for thousands of others to read shows that there was a deep hunger for news about life in their occupied homeland. The *Review* was passed from one evacuee to another (not all could afford to purchase a copy) then sent overseas to be read by Islanders serving in the forces. One issue stated, 'Imagine the pleasure of a Channel Islander in Gibraltar or Egypt, reading familiar names and places.' There was a gap in publication between April and July 1942 due to the 'Control of Paper Order'. The CIRC took the matter to Parliament where Lord Portsea explained the importance of the magazine to Channel Island evacuees, and Islanders in the forces. On 3 June 1942, the Ministry of Supply granted a supply of paper to the *Review* and when the editor was told that the magazine could continue, he stated:

This shows that the Channel Islanders have not been forgotten, and that the friendly welcome so evident and spontaneous two years ago has neither lessened nor grown dim!

This 'friendly welcome' was borne out by the fact that leading local dignitaries frequently attended Channel Island Society meetings. The Mayor of Bolton advised Islanders, 'When peace returns, the islands will be invaded by Lancashire holidaymakers who, having heard so much of the islands, are curious to see them for themselves!' The Mayor of Bury endorsed the local collection of funds

Advertisement for Ritz cinema concert.

RITZ CINEMA

DUKE STREET STOCKPORT   'Phone 4251.

Sunday, Oct. 18, at 7 p.m.
Grand Sunday Evening Entertainment

THE ROYAL COMMAND PERFORMER,

NORMAN EVANS
AMBASSADOR OF MIRTH.

IVOR   DAVE
MORETON & KAYE
THE ORIGINAL TIGER RAG-A-MUFFINS.

JACK KIRKLAND AND HIS BROADCASTING STARS
14 STAR PERFORMERS—Direct from a Tour of Seaside Sunday Concert Successes.

and the Following Guest Artistes:—

BERYL and BERT, A Girl, a Boy and a Guitar!	**GERRY BRERETON** Stockport's Own Vocalist.
JACK GRICE, The North's Own Comedian and Compere.	**JACK LEACH** Wizard of the Ivor Direct from Cocoa Grove, London
CLIFF BURKE, London's Ambassador of Song.	**NELSON FRAN** Manchester's Bri Impressionis

ORGANISED IN AID OF STOCKPORT CHANNEL REFUGEES.

ADMISSION: 5/-, 4/-, 3/-, 2/-,
GET YOUR TICKET NOW—ALL SEATS BOO

Monthly Review, May 1941.

★ ★ ★

GUERNSE

MONTHLY REVIEW
—— of the STOCKPORT & DISTRICT ——
CHANNEL ISLANDS SOCIETY

DERNEY

SARK

No. 1.—MAY, 1941.

FOREWORD.

IN presenting this *Monthly Review* to you all, I commend it as yet another link between Channel Islanders wherever they may be. We all understand and fully appreciate that longing for news that has been so uppermost in our minds since the Evacuation last June, news of home, news of dear ones, news of friends, and not to forget the Islands themselves, a desire that has definitely grown in intensity as the long winter months of silence have slowly passed by; a time when any news of our Islands was received with joy as a ray of sunshine in an atmosphere that was clouded with difficulties as well as smoke.

The formation of the Stockport and District Channel Islands Society was the first step in bridging that chasm of separation, and the Society can well claim to have achieved much success in that direction; many have been helped to face up to their perplexities, to move forward, and carry on with resolve and courage to that day when we return, leaving behind us a standard of living that will be a lasting credit to us, and a glowing tribute to the goodness and kindness bestowed on us by hundreds of welfare workers in England—this dear old Mother Country of ours.

And now this second step, the *Monthly Review*, a tangible way of conveying news to all our friends, relatives, Channel Islanders in the Forces, the Mercantile Marine, perhaps thousands of miles away—who knows. This medium, which is to be published at regular intervals, will contain a record of our activities as a Society and the news that is read out at our various meetings, and will be obtainable at a small cost, just enough to defray the cost of printing.

So it is hoped that this venture will prove a worthy link in further cementing our bonds of friendship and be another means of helping us on with the " daily round and common task," until that day comes for us to take ship, slip down Channel, pass the pier heads to live again in those beautiful sunny islands set in the silver seas, better known as "Home."

Until that day breaks, let us not be weary in well-doing—Good luck and God's blessing to you all from us all.—P.J.M.

Procedure on Sunday Afternoons. 1. Lord's Prayer and hymn, " Absent Friends." 2. Welcome to Visitors. 3. Announcements. 4. News. 5. Tea.

for Channel Island children at Christmas. Lady Astor distributed Christmas presents to children at several Channel Island Society parties. A Channel Island Rally held at Belle Vue, Manchester, in 1943 was attended by the Deputy Mayor of Manchester. The Mayor of Barnsley was President of the Barnsley Society, and when the Exeter Society held a conference in January 1941, it was attended by the Mayor and Sheriff of Exeter.

Annual reunions and numerous mass meetings brought together Channel Island evacuees from many areas to share their experiences, concerns, and hopes for the future. Edward Searson was chairman of the Manchester Channel Island Society, and his son John recalled:

> The Islanders met once a fortnight on a Sunday in the CWS (Co-operative Wholesale Society) building in Manchester. Besides trips to the seaside and other social events, he organised two large rallies at Belle Vue Stadium, Manchester. One took place in June 1943 and was featured on *Pathé News* and shown in cinemas in the UK. The other took place in 1945 and 6,000 Channel Island refugees attended from all over Britain.

The Halifax Society held a reunion on Boxing Day 1941 which was attended by 160 evacuees. Mass meetings were held on 21, 22 and 23 February 1942 in Bradford, Bolton and Stockport, with over 1,000 present at Bolton's impressive Albert Hall. In August 1942, 200 members of the Stockport Society were met at Bolton station by members of the Bolton Society, then they all walked in a long crocodile to a local hall. In June 1943, evacuees attended a Confederation of Channel Island Societies in London, and a rally was held at Westminster Central Hall that same month.

Channel Island Society committees organised joint conferences too, and Percy Martel's diary contains tickets and notes relating to those which he attended. An argument broke out at one London conference when committee members met with representatives from the CIRC, the Home Office and the Ministry of Health. A member from the Exeter Channel Island Society stated that he would like to publish 'a Channel Island magazine which would incorporate news and items from all the societies, to be edited and controlled in London or some other centre.' Another member felt the Stockport society was in fact 'running its *Review* paper under false pretences, because a Channel Islands paper should be in the hands of a body duly elected by every Channel Island Society!' There were angry exchanges which were interrupted by a gentleman who congratulated Stockport on their initiative in starting a magazine. The vice-chairman brought an end to the discussion, stating this matter would be looked into at a later date, and that 'there must be no quarrel among Channel Islanders.' The last major gathering in the north-west of England was probably the Joint Conference of

STADIUM BELLE VUE MANCHESTER

CHANNEL ISLANDERS
COMMEMORATION RALLY
SATURDAY, 19TH JUNE, 1943, AT 2-30 P.M.

ENTRANCE—STADIUM GATE, HYDE ROAD,
Hunters Lane Corner. (Open 2 p.m.)

Visitors from Manchester direction travelling
by tramcar should alight at Birch Street.

Free admission to Belle Vue Gardens after conclusion of Rally.

This ticket to be given up on entering the Stadium.

Belle Vue rally entrance ticket.

Channel Island Societies on 14 April 1945 in Huddersfield Town Hall. The liberation of the Channel Islands, and plans for returning home, were the top items for discussion.

The Channel Island societies were important to the Guernsey evacuees, but in addition they frequently visited each other's homes, or called into the Guernsey schools. Headmaster Percy Martel described this as 'a touch with home, spreading goodwill, comfort and cheer, reviving the Channel Island spirit and helping to bridge the gap in our lives.' Rhona Le Page recalls:

Throughout the war, Mum was constantly dragging me from one relative's home to another, usually on foot as we could not afford bus fares much. She could not seem to sit still, but had to keep up the visiting, either she went to them or they came to us! And her first words were always 'Do you have any news from home?' Sometimes she was bitterly disappointed.

In March 1941 Muriel Parsons met some of the female schoolteachers who had arrived in Cheshire, and having brought her camera with her from Guernsey, she took a photograph of them. The evacuees' diaries describe with delight the visits they received from family and friends. Hazel Hall wrote, 'Today my brother Rex, who is now in the army, visited me, bringing with him my younger brother Ken whose school is in Cheshire. It was a lovely surprise and we had a photograph taken!' Ruth Alexandre noted in her diary:

DELEGATE'S ADMISSION TICKET **91**

TO

Joint Conference of
Channel Islands Societies

AT

The Town Hall, Huddersfield,

ON

Saturday, April 14th, 1945

commencing 3 p.m.

Name .... **Mr. P.J.Martel.** ....

From (state Town in England)....... STOCKPORT.........

PLEASE ENTER THE TOWN HALL BY
THE CORPORATION STREET ENTRANCE

Admission to Conference and Tea by Ticket only

Ticket for the Channel Island conference.

October 21st – met up with lots of the adults for a long chat, and then visited Connie in Crawshawbooth, on 22nd went to Ruth's, Nellie came to my home in the afternoon, then later Mr Creighton popped round, on 28th Ruth came to tea, Fred turned up too, I went to Auntie Flo's later, then went to Channel Island Society committee meeting at 6.30 p.m.

Paulette Le Mescam's school received visits from Guernsey soldiers who were home on leave. The boys of Elizabeth College received visits from ex-pupils who were either at English universities, or in the forces. In September 1941 around 200 of the college's ex-pupils were enlisted in the forces, and one month they received visits from eighteen ex-pupils, including F.G. Caldwell who was on leave from service in Egypt. They were saddened to hear of the death of two ex-pupils, who had both been killed in action.[2]

During the war the police monitored the movements of foreigners or 'aliens' to ensure that they were not spies or saboteurs. The public were warned about talking to 'strangers', and those who spoke a foreign language were often treated with suspicion. Evacuees and refugees had to advise the authorities if they wanted to visit another area. In December 1941, Muriel Parsons visited St Ives where she was arrested on suspicion of being a spy:

Hazel, Ken and Rex Hall.

M.ʳ HOLMAN. M.ʳˢ LE PELLY   M.ⁱˢˢ CLAYTON
M.ʳ NAFTEL   M.ⁱˢˢ JONES   M.ʳˢ BARLOW

Muriel Parsons' photograph of Guernsey teachers.

I had to explain my purpose in Cornwall, why I didn't speak North Countryish, why I was carrying a camera. How were they to know I wasn't a spy, come over with the evacuees from Guernsey, and with whom was I staying and for how long? Golly, wasn't it funny – but rather annoying when I found I had missed the shops!

After that episode, Muriel applied for a permit whenever she visited other areas. Her diary contains a letter from Portsmouth police, advising her that she had permission to visit the town without a permit. In June 1940, the *Daily Mirror* had published an article entitled, 'If Strangers ask you, don't tell!' A number of the Guernsey evacuees spoke 'Guernsey patois', based on Norman French, and Margaret Duquemin recalls that her mother occasionally spoke patois to other evacuees:

> Passers-by would give her odd looks, I was scared that they would think that we were German, and although only seven years old, I would walk behind her, ready to run for help if needed, or escape.

Suzanne Lang's mother occasionally whispered some patois, usually when she wanted to keep her thoughts secret from the people around her. Anne Le Noury recalled one particular incident that took place on a bus when her mother spoke Guernsey patois:

> A man asked Mum what language we were speaking. She explained and he advised her (saying he was with the CID) to teach us to converse only in English. Wise advice as we experienced some hostile treatment from a minority of neighbours. Situations flared up – sometimes related to the latest wartime bulletins. There might be swastikas drawn on the doors or we'd be told to 'Go home dirty Germans'.

An aspect of Guernsey culture that is reflected in evacuees' diaries and letters, and copies of Stockport's *Review,* was the singing of traditional Island songs and the writing of poems. Most of the poems described the evacuation, the constant thoughts of Guernsey, and the eventual return. Joan Ozanne's poem which describes her leaving Guernsey is included at the beginning of chapter one. In June 1942, Irene Guille wrote a poem to mark the second anniversary of the evacuation to England, part of which read:

> Through joys and through trials,
> Through weeks, months or years,
> Till victorious at last we shall be;
> And those very same ships
> That brought us to these shores
> Take us back to the isles o'er the seas
>
> When we shall meet again,
> Those whom God has preserved
> For that long-looked for, grand future day;
> And together we'll stand
> On the cliffs and the sand,
> And we'll thank Him who showed us the way.

Another evacuee wrote:

> The waving hands, the eager word, the welcoming call
> When those long parted are restored – and free.

The Stockport *Review* printed another:

> The sun is warm again on English hills and dales
> And wakes to life the Scottish brakes and braes
> But still we dream of Guernsey's emerald fields and vales
> The jade and pearl of Sarnia's sheltered bays,
> In dreams we hear the gentle waves caress the shore,
> We scent the fragrance of the laden breeze
> We see the cliffs all gleaming brightly as of yore
> A blaze of gold above the silver sea.

Traditional Channel Island songs were also very popular, and evacuees in Bury sang Guernsey and Jersey songs at their Channel Island Society meetings. One mother recalled, 'We sang "Sarnia Cherie" and my eyes filled with tears. In my mind, I could see my Guernsey home and my husband as I sang.'

Muriel Parsons described a concert given by the Guernsey Girls Intermediate School in Rochdale as 'very good indeed' and pasted the concert programme into her diary. Percy Martel described a party where 'Our children gave us "Sarnia Cherie", our lovely Guernsey song, which the WVS ladies enjoyed and which made my heart proud.' 'Sarnia Cherie' had been sung in Guernsey prior to the evacuation, but during the war it became especially important. It was sung at many Channel Island Society meetings, and became the anthem of the Guernsey evacuees both during and after the war because of its poignant lyrics:

> Sarnia Cherie, Gem of the sea
> Home of my childhood, my heart longs for thee
> Thy voice calls me ever, Forget thee, I'll never
> Island of Beauty, Sarnia Cherie

Before the war, the Church had been important to Guernsey people, and it continued to be so for the evacuees. They found comfort there, together with an opportunity to meet other evacuees and to befriend local people. Reta Batiste wrote:

> It was not long before we found a place where we were not 'strangers in a strange land' – the local Methodist church. We made good friends amongst the members, many of whom helped us knowing of the poor allowance we received.

STATES INTERMEDIATE SCHOOL. GUERNSEY

Programme

1. Song of Welcome .... The Junior School.

2. {Two French Songs   1. Verduron
                         2. Petronille.

   {Two Guernsey Songs   1. Gros Jean
                         2. Le jour du lavage

3. Folk Songs of many   1. Ma Normandie
   Lands.   2. Fisherman's
                            Evening Song.
                         3. Morning in
                            Tyrol.
                         4. In a gondola
                         5. Santa Lucia
                         6. Polish National
                            Dance.

4. Two piano solos on   1. Hungarian Dance
   Characteristic   No.5.   Brahms.
   Dance Rhythms.   2. Valse No. 11
                            Chopin.   W. Roughton.

5. Junior   1. Shoes & Stockings   Form 1.
   Recitations.   2. The Flower Seller   Forms 11. 111.
                         3. The Middle-sized   Forms 11. 111.
                            Bear.   and V111.

   Country Dances
6. English   1. Black Nag   Forms Up.1V.V.
                         2. We won't go home
                            till morning.   Form Low 1V.
                         3. Grimstock   Form Low VI.

   Scandinavian.   1. Clap Dance
                         2. Cochin China   Upper V1
   Irish   JIG   LOWER IV
7. Junior Acted   The Princess on   Forms 11.111.
   Song.   the hill of Glass.   Up.111

8. Violin Solos   Selected   N.H.Roughton

9. Two Classical   1. Cradle Song
   Songs.   2. The Blacksmith   Brahms.

   Four British   1. All through the Night.
   Songs.   2. The Lass of Richmond
                            Hill.
                         3. Rolling Down to Rio. Edward German
                         4. The Forward Road.

10. The Guernsey
    Song.   Sarnia Chérie   Santangelo

                GOD SAVE THE KING.

Concert programme, Intermediate School, Rochdale.

95

NAME *Master Robert H. Langlois*

FOR TODAY: to remind you of the Infinite Love watching over our loved ones and ourselves : to acknowledge with thanksgiving that we have found kindly friends as well as hardship in our time of exile: and—

FOR THE COMING DAYS: the remembrance that even this time of distress has brought its own enriching experience, not yet to be measured or understood :

THIS BOOK, the greatest in the world, is sent to bring to you its own word of strength, and "Grace to help in time of need."

With affectionate greetings
Your sincere friends

R. D. Moore

G. Whitley

January 1941.
1 Central Buildings,
Westminster, S.W.1.

Robert Langlois' bible.

Davenport Methodist Church noted several new Guernsey members in its congregation; the Fallas and the Collinettes, while the Church Roll Book mentions the attendance of the Brehaut family.[3] Guernsey's Revd R.D. Moore, wrote about the evacuees in *The Methodist Recorder*, and travelled around Britain, offering comfort to the evacuees, and presenting them with New Testaments. Ruth Alexandre wrote in her diary 'Reverend Moore came to our meeting and seems to have caused a sensation!' His visits gave the evacuees a connection to their island, to its church, and to other evacuees throughout Britain. The Revd George Whiteley had been a Superintendent of the Guernsey Methodist Circuit, and in England he was appointed to assist the evacuees from a church office at Central Hall, Westminster. In one month alone he visited the CIRC in London, the Forest School in Cheshire, the Elizabeth College boys in Derbyshire, the Intermediate School in Oldham and meetings of the Croydon and the Stockport Channel Island societies. During his visit to the Elizabeth College, he advised the boys, 'Remember that the Channel Islanders will be judged in this country by their behaviour. You must not let the islands down.'

Special church services were frequently arranged for Channel Islanders, and in one month alone, services were held in Horsforth, St Helens, Stockport, Barnsley and Halifax. In 1943, a service was led by the Bishop of Middleton at Manchester Cathedral. The evacuees also received the constant support of the Bishop of Winchester during the war, because the Channel Islands were within his jurisdiction. In January 1943 hundreds of Channel Islanders flocked to a service at St Martin-in-the-Fields, London, which was led by the Archbishop of York. The hymns were particularly relevant to the plight of the evacuees' families in Guernsey. One included the words 'Keep our loved ones, now far distant, Neath thy care . . . When in sorrow, when in danger, in Thy love look down and comfort their distress.' Later, the *Review* reported that:

> The rendition of this particular hymn was not good, for we sang with tears and there was grief and sorrow in our hearts, for in that moment we were conscious of another parting from those with whom and for whom we had prayed for so brief a space.[4]

Percy and Muriel Rowland attended a Channel Islands service at Westminster Abbey in April 1944, and their son, Sir Geoffrey Rowland, still possesses their entrance ticket. 2,000 people managed to obtain seats, while large numbers stood, and Stockport's *Review* described the address which was led by the Dean of Westminster:

> It was a day of tragedy indeed, not only for you, but also for us in England . . . when the Germans landed and took possession of your towns and villages

. . . for when all is said and done, your islands are the oldest possession of the British Crown . . . by your spirit of deathless courage and indomitable hope, you have made a real contribution to our national morale. May God hasten the day when you shall return to your homes.

Churches often provided venues for Channel Island Society meetings, either free of charge or for a small hire fee. Peter Rouxel's mother was on the committee of the Nantwich society which met at the Methodist Church Schoolroom on Hospital Street, Nantwich. The Bury society held meetings at the local Temperance Hall, while from 1941 the Stockport society met at Tiviot Dale Methodist Church. At Tiviot Dale, the Revd Mark Lund became the evacuees' chaplain for the whole of the war. So close was their relationship, that when the evacuees prepared to return to Guernsey in 1945, they donated £78 to the Church Trust Fund. The Revd Lund decided to go back with them to Guernsey, and he was duly stationed at St Peter Port Methodist Church.

Some of the evacuated Guernsey Catholic schools held their own private services. Paulette Le Mescam wrote, 'Here in Moseley Hall we have Mass here every morning, and Holy Communion whenever we want it.' The senior boys of Elizabeth College moved into a large house, Whitehall, near Buxton, where they slept on the floor until the Red Cross provided them with iron bedsteads. They discovered that the premises contained a neglected chapel, which they quickly renovated. The college principal wrote at the time, 'This chapel, largely controlled by a committee of boys, has become a vital centre for the whole

NORTH CHOIR AISLE

Westminster Abbey

A SERVICE

FOR

CHANNEL ISLANDS REFUGEES NOW RESIDENT IN ENGLAND

ON

Sunday, April 30th, 1944, at 3 p.m.

Entrance
By the Great West Door

PAUL DE LABILLIERE, *Dean.*

Ticket Holders are requested to be seated by not later than 2.45 p.m.

Westminster Abbey ticket.

Elizabeth College's wartime chapel.

communal life.' Vernon Collenette wrote, 'A table was procured and one of the boys made a simple wooden cross for the altar. Each day until the end of the war we had prayers, and a service each Sunday.'

To this day, the college proudly displays this wooden cross in the entrance hall in Guernsey.

Images of the Channel Islands themselves were very much in demand during the war. Books, films and photographs were taken to Channel Island Society meetings and to evacuees' homes. Ted Reade found a Channel Island holiday guide on a Bradford market stall, and recalled, 'as the years passed, the photographs in that book were worth more to us than all the pictures in the National Gallery.'[5] Films of the Islands were eagerly distributed around the Channel Island network – the Southern Railway Publicity Department had made an advertising film of the islands just before the war and this was extremely popular. A large group of evacuees visited the Elysian Theatre where a film about Guernsey was being shown, and Percy Martel later wrote, 'The views of Guernsey proceeded in quick succession in a silence that could be felt, that portrayed the feeling that existed in the hearts of these people.'

A film shown at one well-attended meeting resulted in a member writing 'it is a great sight to watch 325 Islanders all weeping heartily at films of their country.'

The evacuees keenly followed the progress of the war through the *Pathé News* bulletins, the radio and the press, and diaries contain press cuttings on the war's advances and set-backs. When the evacuees learned that Channel Islanders were being deported from Guernsey, they now had three things to worry about – those on the island, those who were fighting in the forces, and those who had been deported. Channel Island societies, the British Red Cross and the Channel Islands Refugee Committee sent 'next of kin' parcels, containing personal items and clothing, to Islanders in German camps. In April 1942, members of Guernsey's police force were arrested in connection with thefts from German food stores. Rose Duquemin's father, Sergeant Fred Duquemin, was among these officers, and Rose recalls:

> They were caught and had confessions beaten out of them, and were made to sign documents which were written in German. They did not know what they had signed until they were in court. They pleaded guilty as they could hardly say that they were doing their bit against the enemy – that would have earned them a death sentence. Dad was charged with receiving, and his sentence was 2 years 6 months hard labour.

Rose's mother, Nell, eventually managed to contact her husband through the British Red Cross, and a note sent by Fred in October 1943 finally reached Nell in March 1944:

> Dear Nell just a few lines hoping they will find you and all the children in the best of health, as for myself I am A1 and working every day in the laundry . . . please send me a photo of children and yourself . . . Love to all from Fred.

Fred served three years, before being liberated from the camp by American forces, and Rose's family suddenly discovered that Fred was due to arrive in England:

> All Dad knew of our whereabouts was that in June 1940 we were in Stockport, Cheshire . . . they contacted the Stockport police, who visited pubs and other public places looking for Channel Islanders, and asking them if they knew Mum. They eventually found us and it was arranged that we would meet him at a house in London. We knocked on the door and Dad answered it. I did not recognise him but I knew it was him because Mum threw her arms around him.

The family set off to take Fred back to their home in Stockport, and took a taxi across London to reach the railway station. Rose recalls:

When Mum paid our fare she gave the taxi driver a small tip, he did not think it was enough and he threw it back at her and told us that buses were good enough for the likes of us. Dad looked like a tramp, he had lost a lot of weight . . . he was wearing an old raincoat with box cord instead of a belt. The driver said that his son was in Germany fighting and the likes of us were riding in taxis. Mum soon gave him a piece of her mind and told him why we needed to ride in a taxi.

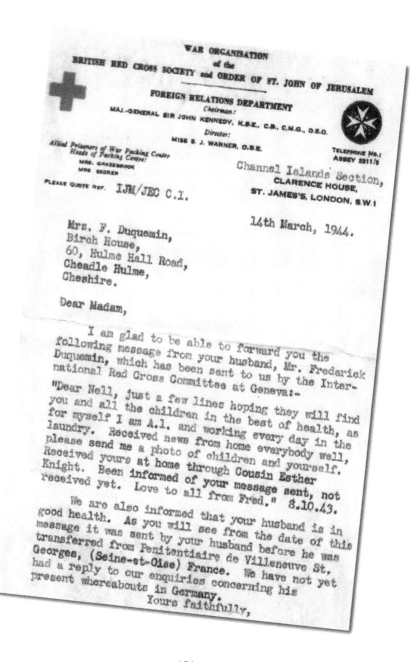

Mr and Mrs Remfrey had sent their two eldest children to England in June 1940, but the rest of the family did not leave because their youngest child was too ill to travel. Later, the rest of the family, including their children, Anne, Tommy, Jimmy, and Michael, were deported to Germany. Maureen Dorrian was evacuated to England but two of her brothers remained in Guernsey and were deported to a camp at Biberach with their wives. When they were eventually released, they lived with Maureen until they were able to return to Guernsey.

In contrast, the evacuees' morale was given a boost when they heard of Islanders who had escaped from Guernsey under the very noses of the Germans. Several future film and television actors were among the Guernsey families which escaped, including Roy Dotrice, and *Coronation Street*'s John Savident who played the much-loved character Fred Elliot. The Savident family was one of the first families to escape, leaving Guernsey on 1 July 1940, the day after the island was occupied. Mr and Mrs Savident brought their three children, John (aged three), Joseph and Cyril, to England, and John recalls:

> We came to Huddersfield first and then Ashton where I grew up. My family spoke Channel Islands French patois, a kind of dialect – but we had to learn to speak English very quickly or we'd always be marked as different.[6]

British Family in German Prison

Anne, Tommy and Jimmy Remfry, with their baby brother Michael, who was not born when this picture was taken three years ago, have been moved with their parents, Mr. and Mrs. T. A. Remfry, of Tunbridge Wells, to a German prison camp, Stalag VI.F.

Staying behind in Guernsey to nurse Anne, who was ill when the Germans invaded the Island, they missed the last boat, in which the elder children, Donald, now 13, and Pat (10), sailed to England.

★

A card which left Germany on October 17 told Pat and Don, now staying with their grandmother at Tunbridge Wells, that "all arrived safely, fairly well."

"We know we have another little brother," said Pat yesterday. "We think he was born two years ago.

"Anne is six now, Tommy nine, and Jimmy seven. The ship's doctor told daddy that Anne would die if she came with us."

On 14 August 1943, William Corbet escaped Guernsey in the *Kate*, an 18ft motor dinghy, with four men and three women. The fact that William had been a ship's engineer during the First World War enabled him to escape Guernsey successfully. He managed to evade several German E-boats in the Channel, and his boat was eventually stopped by a Royal Navy minesweeper. William went aboard to speak to the crew while hot drinks, chocolate and cigarettes were lowered to the other passengers. Upon arriving in England, William was able to give the authorities information about troop numbers and living conditions in Guernsey, including the fact that many shops were running short of stock. He also met the Channel Islands Refugee Committee, and spoke at several Channel Island Society meetings in England. In Guernsey, William's parents were arrested and questioned, fishing was halted for a time, and islanders were forbidden to venture onto beaches. From then on, the property of those that escaped was confiscated by the occupying forces.[7]

In April 1944, Harry Ingrouille and another man escaped from Alderney in a motorised fishing boat, the *Ottawa*, after hoarding fuel for some time. They had been sent from Guernsey to Alderney to provide fish for German troops on the island. A guard was supposed to accompany the fishermen each day, but on the day of his planned escape, Harry told the guard that the presence of a German in the boat might attract the attention of a British Spitfire and they would all be killed. Upon arriving in Weymouth, the men were taken into custody and transferred to London for interview. After their release they made visits to Guernsey evacuees, including the Ozanne family in Croydon and Joan Ozanne recalls, 'it was my birthday and his visit was a wonderful present.' Harry later paid a visit to Percy Martel's Guernsey school which had been re-established in Cheshire, and Percy noted in his diary:

> This visit was a marvel, yes a marvel! He went into every classroom, and the children's names were called, one by one. 'Yes I saw your father and mother just before I left, they are well,' 'Your parents are living at . . .', 'Your father is working at . . .' and so on. One boy asked, 'We had a litter of pigs at our house before I left. Are they still alive?' to which Mr I replied, 'No, we have eaten them!' He gave us lots of detailed information about the island and then had lunch with us.

Harry told a reporter:

> Some time ago the RAF dropped half a dozen newspapers on Guernsey, we got to them before the Germans could lay hands on them. They were passed from home to home throughout the island until about 6,000 people had read them.

In Guernsey, Anne Le Noury's father helped two men to escape, but Anne has never discovered their identity. Her mother travelled to London to identify the men, who gave her messages from her husband, but she was told by the authorities not to discuss the matter with anyone.

During the war, the Guernsey flag became an important symbol to the evacuees, representing not just those who had been evacuated from their island, but also the occupied. Some adults also felt that it would be useful to be actually identified as 'Channel Islanders' as they went about their daily business in England. Mrs F. Lucy wrote to the *Review* in July 1942, asking:

Wartime Channel Island badge.
(Image reproduced from No Cause for Panic:
Channel Island Refugees 1940–45 *by Brian*
Ahier Read, Seaflower Books, 1995)

Is it feasible for us to have a badge? A lady and I travelled together over 30 miles on the same bus and never knew we were fellow Islanders until the end . . . if only we had worn a badge!

Another evacuee wrote, 'I have only lately discovered some fellow Islanders. If we had only known before! We should have some button to wear.' The Barnsley society ordered several hundred metal badges at a cost of 11 pence each, and other societies followed suit. The CIRC's accounts for 1944 suggest that around 800 badges had been bought during that year alone. The Croydon Society presented every member with a badge, which depicted their particular island of origin, while the committee members were given their own distinctive badges. Even today, many Channel Islanders wear a pin badge of the Guernsey flag when visiting friends and family in England.

NOTES

1   Brian Ahier Read, *No Cause for Panic*, p. 91

2   *Elizabethan Magazine*, February 1941, p. 22.

3   Stockport Heritage Library Archives, D1406, Davenport Methodist Church papers.

4   *Channel Islands Monthly Review*, Special Bulletin, February 1943, p. 4.

5   Brian Read Archive, testimony of Ted Reade, undated.

6   *Manchester Evening News*, 18 May 2011, interview with John Savident.

7   Christian Cardell Corbet, Corbet Family Channel Islands Collection, the escape of William Corbet.

4

THE KINDNESS OF STRANGERS

I didn't have any communication with members of my own family throughout the whole of the war. It was so lovely to receive letters and parcels from someone who cared about me.[1]

Surviving wartime records show there were certain individuals and organisations which made a huge difference to the lives of the evacuees, not just financially, but also emotionally. This chapter will take a look at four of these: Mrs Eleanor Roosevelt, the Foster Parent Plan for War Children, the Canadian Channel Islanders' Societies, and the efforts of Mr John W. Fletcher, an elderly resident of Bury, Lancashire.

ELEANOR ROOSEVELT AND THE FOSTER PARENT PLAN

As mentioned in chapter three, some of the evacuated Guernsey schools were re-established in England, in order to keep the children and teachers together until the end of the war. One of these schools was La Chaumière Catholic School, but the school only survived because it received financial help from the 'Foster Parent Plan for Children Affected by War' (FPP). One of the supporters of the FPP was Mrs Eleanor Roosevelt, the wife of the President of the United States of America.

In June 1940, the pupils of La Chaumière School had arrived in England under the care of Father Bleach, and three nuns, Mother Emmanuel and Sisters

*Eleanor Roosevelt (left) with
Mrs Churchill.*

Dennis Archer.

Adolph and Ezear. The school was sent to Eccles and housed in a ballroom with other Guernsey children. Dennis Archer recalled, 'Within a few days, three of us caught 'flu, and because we were all crowded together in the dance hall, we were put in the local hospital. There we were treated like royalty; it was wonderful!'

In early July the staff and pupils of La Chaumière were moved to Knutsford, Cheshire, where they were split up and billeted with local families. However, Father Bleach wanted to keep his staff and students together, and to reopen his school in England. After searching for several months, he found Moseley Hall, a large empty mansion with beautiful grounds and two tennis courts. The Hall's owner, Mr Stuttart, was living in Wales at the time, and decided to give the building to Father Bleach rent-free, rather than have it taken over by troops. It was wonderful for the children to be reunited with their school friends and teachers under the same roof. They were soon joined by Mrs Merrien, her baby son Dick, and sixteen-year-old daughter Beryl. Beryl recalled:

We had been evacuated to Glasgow at first, and Father Bleach wrote to my mum to ask her if we would like to join him at Moseley Hall. Some of our family were pupils there. He said that Mum and I would need to do some work, and that he wouldn't be able to pay us any wages or pocket money at present, but at least we would have food and shelter, and all be together as a family.

In common with the other Guernsey teachers who re-established their schools in England, Father Bleach faced severe financial difficulties. He spent weeks tracking down beds, linen, toys and equipment by begging at factories, local authorities and warehouses, and made frequent visits to the Red Cross offices in London. However, the school's fortunes changed for the better when Father Bleach discovered the existence of the 'Foster Parent Plan for Children Affected by War' (FPP). The FPP had been founded in 1937 by two friends – John Langdon-Davies, a journalist, and Eric Muggeridge, a social worker, and the brother of author and journalist Malcolm Muggeridge. The original aims of the FPP were to help children whose lives had been disrupted by the Spanish Civil War. On more than one occasion, Eric Muggeridge had led groups of terrified children across the freezing snowbound passes of the Pyrenees to the French border. Sadly, the cold and snow and incessant bombings ended the journey for many of the children.

In 1939 the FPP became a chartered New York organisation so that it had access to fundraising opportunities in the United States, and began to help children from all countries whose lives were being affected by the Second World War. The FPP letterhead was amended to include the motto, 'To help children of the UN and the little victims of Nazi oppression receive food, shelter and loving care through the Foster Parent Plan'.

Moseley Hall, Knutsford.

The FPP set up committees in England and America which began to enlist people who would contribute financially to the support of children, and become their 'foster parents'. In England, people were asked to donate 1s a day to provide a child with food and shelter. They were also asked to write letters to the child to show that someone cared about them – creating what we now call 'child sponsorship'. Eric Muggeridge's daughter, Maureen, recalled:

> My father used to talk in front of huge crowds of well-off Americans, pleading for sponsors for these suffering children. He obviously did quite well to attract some very well-known people who are proudly displayed on the Sponsor List. He was very persuasive about the things he was passionate about, none more so than helping desperate children.

Eric was clearly very persuasive, as the list of FPP sponsors includes some well-known names from the 1940s. Sponsors in England and America included Bing Crosby, Jack Benny, Dean Martin, J.B. Priestley and Dame Sybil Thorndike. The FPP also established 'colonies' in England to provide children with financial and emotional assistance, and the Guernsey children of La Chaumière School now became one of the FPP's 'colonies'. Beryl Merrien helped the children to write letters to their foster parents, and on occasion she attached photographs of the children. Pearl Saltwell received letters, parcels, a school yearbook and chewing gum from her sponsors – students at Tranquility Union High School in California. Sponsored children sometimes received enough money for tea parties to be arranged at La Chaumière. Mavis Fitzpatrick bought cakes for all the children with the birthday gift of five dollars she received from Mrs Joseph Harchow of Columbus, Ohio.

In November 1942, Eleanor Roosevelt, the wife of the American President Franklin D. Roosevelt, visited the London headquarters of the FPP. Eleanor despised social injustice and had a great sensitivity to the underprivileged of all races, creeds and nations. She decided to sponsor three children, one of whom was Paulette Le Mescam at La Chaumière School. Paulette became 'Foster child 306' to Mrs Eleanor Roosevelt who was 'Foster Parent 200'. Soon after, Eleanor received a brief summary of Paulette's life, together with details of her character, and a photograph:

> Paulette is about five feet tall and is in fine health. She is fond of school, and does especially well in Religious Instruction and English. Her French is, of course, very good. She is fond of singing, and is almost always humming as merry tune![2]

Paulette Le Mescam holding a toy bus.

Prior to receiving letters and parcels from Mrs Roosevelt, Paulette had not heard from her own parents for over five years. Paulette had been born in Paris in 1932, but when she was only eighteen months old, her mother had died. Her father, Yves Le Mescam, was a member of the Free French who chose to fight against the Nazis after the surrender of France. This prevented him from caring for Paulette and her sister, Monique, and in 1936 he sent Paulette to live with her maternal grandmother in Guernsey. In June 1940, Paulette had been evacuated with La Chaumière School and lived in three different billets in Knutsford. In the first billet, the family did not seem to care for her at all:

> I felt that they just wanted the billeting allowance. They never took me anywhere with them. If they went out, I had to sit on the doorstep until they came home as I wasn't allowed into the house on my own. One day they did not return until 10 p.m.

Paulette was happy in her third billet with a Mrs Ballatine, 'She was lovely and wanted to adopt me, but if course it was not allowed.' When Father Bleach obtained the use of Moseley Hall for La Chaumière's pupils, Paulette was happy to be reunited with her Guernsey friends and teachers.

When Paulette began writing to Mrs Roosevelt and receiving letters from the White House, neither the name nor the address meant anything to her – 'I was only 11 years old at the time and of course there was no television in those days, so we didn't hear a lot about famous people. To me, she was just my "Aunty Eleanor".'

Mrs Roosevelt provided Father Bleach with 10s a week for Paulette's care, together with letters, and parcels which often included clothing. Paulette recalls the excitement of receiving the parcels from America, which bore the distinctive Foster Parent Plan label – 'She sent me some lovely clothes. I particularly remember receiving some Lux soap which had a lovely smell, and a lovely red dress.'

Paulette was delighted to receive letters from Mrs Roosevelt, as she received no communication from anyone else throughout the war. Paulette's first letter to Mrs Roosevelt described her life in Knutsford:

> We are living in one big house altogether. Moseley Hall is a beautiful house and it was given to us by a kind man. My mother is dead and my father is a sailor. I do not know where he is now. My sister is somewhere in France but I do not know where . . . God bless you and keep you safe. Your loving foster child, Paulette.

In April 1943 Paulette described the Easter celebrations taking place at school, and included an Easter drawing for Mrs Roosevelt – the first of many drawings

*The Foster Parent
Plan parcel tag.*

sent to her sponsor. Eric Muggeridge now realised that Eleanor Roosevelt's sponsorship of Paulette could focus public attention on the work of the FPP, and he invited Paulette to speak with him on BBC radio. Now Paulette discovered who 'Aunty Eleanor' actually was. In May 1943, Eric and Paulette visited London where they watched the changing of the guard at Buckingham Palace and delivered a radio broadcast at the BBC. Paulette spoke in both French and English about the work of the FPP and about her sponsor, Mrs Roosevelt, who was actually listening to the broadcast. Just prior to the broadcast, Paulette was interviewed by the press and asked what she would say on air that afternoon. She told them, 'I don't know what I shall say, but I will tell them about my father as he is a prisoner of war. I have not seen him for a long time.' After the BBC broadcast photographers began to come to Moseley Hall to photograph and interview Paulette and the other children.

In her next letter, Paulette addressed her sponsor as 'Dear Mrs Roosevelt', adding, 'I hope you are in good health. Please give my best regards to President Roosevelt. I heard you speak on the wireless, you speak very well and very plain. I understood every word you said.'

In October 1943, Eleanor Roosevelt was annoyed to discover that Paulette had received a dress which was too large for her. She instructed her secretary to write a letter to the FPP's head office in New York:

Paulette and Eric Muggeridge at the BBC.

It seems to Mrs Roosevelt that the method of selecting clothes for these children might be improved if, as this child states, the dress sent her is so large that she must wait to grow up to wear it. This seems to Mrs Roosevelt inefficient and foolish.

Two days later, the executive chairman of the FPP replied:

In checking our records we find that Paulette, who is small for her age, received a size sixteen dress, instead of a twelve. It was certainly never meant that a child should receive a dress so large that she would have to put it away until she grew into it. We regret very much that this should have happened in connection with Mrs Roosevelt's gift for Paulette and are having the correct size sent to the child at once.

In January 1944 Paulette thanked Mrs Roosevelt for a Christmas parcel containing a green dress, a blouse, a warm red cardigan and a red velvet frock. Thankfully, Paulette also mentioned that 'the Sister altered the red velvet frock so it fits just nicely.' In April 1944 Mrs Roosevelt sent another parcel of clothing to Paulette, consisting of two dresses, a muslin slip, pyjamas and socks. That same month Paulette's letter to Mrs Roosevelt was partly censored, but ended with the heartfelt words:

> I hope this dreadful war will soon be over so that I may return to my beloved native home Paris, with my father and sister, then I could tell them how kind you have been to me. Thanking you over and over again for your kindness to a poor helpless refugee from Guernsey. Your loving foster child, Paulette.

FPP Gift to Foster Child receipt.

113

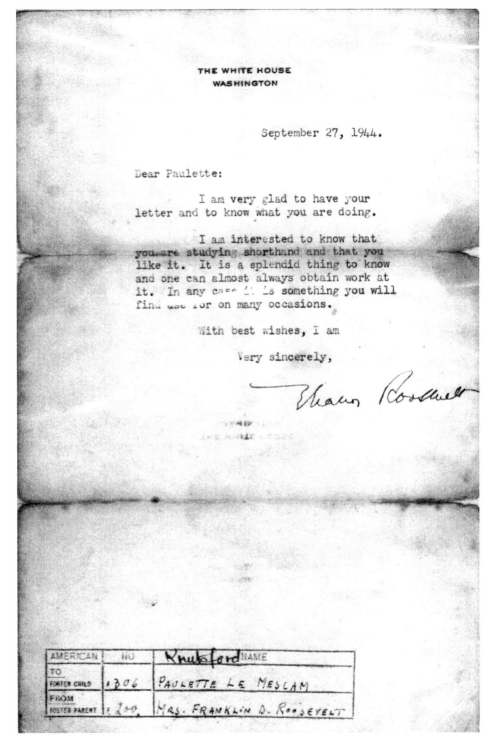

THE WHITE HOUSE
WASHINGTON

September 27, 1944.

Dear Paulette:

I am very glad to have your
letter and to know what you are doing.

I am interested to know that
you are studying shorthand and that you
like it. It is a splendid thing to know
and one can almost always obtain work at
it. In any case it is something you will
find use for on many occasions.

With best wishes, I am

Very sincerely,

Eleanor Roosevelt

AMERICAN	NO	Knutsford NAME
TO FOSTER CHILD	#306	PAULETTE LE MESCAM
FROM FOSTER PARENT	F 200.	MRS. FRANKLIN D. ROOSEVELT

Letter from Eleanor Roosevelt.

Two months later, Paulette told Mrs Roosevelt that the evacuees were marking the fourth anniversary of their evacuation to England and that, because of the recent invasion of Normandy, they had received 'the happy news that we could write long letters to Guernsey and tell them about ourselves.' However, it was to be almost another year before the islands were liberated and they could write to Guernsey. In 1944, Paulette began to learn shorthand from Beryl Merrien. Somehow she obtained a picture postcard of Guernsey and sent it to Mrs Roosevelt, with the message:

> Dear Aunty Eleanor I am sending this beautiful view to show you how pretty our little island is. We are all waiting to return and see all these beautiful places again. I have now started shorthand and I like it very much. We have a lesson every night.

Paulette still has the letter that Mrs Roosevelt sent to her in reply in September 1944. Mrs Roosevelt encouraged Paulette to persevere with her shorthand lessons, saying 'It is a splendid thing to know, and one can almost always obtain work in it.'

That same month Paulette told Eleanor that the whole school had been singing anthems, including 'God Save our Gracious King', and 'The Star Spangled Banner'. Around this time, the owner of Moseley Hall decided to sell the property, but he made a provision in the contract for the children to remain there until they could return to Guernsey. After 9 May 1945 when the Channel Islands had been liberated, the children and staff of La Chaumière began to prepare for their return to Guernsey. Paulette received a final letter from Mrs Roosevelt which included an invitation to visit the White House. However, Paulette was unable to accept this offer, 'I was only young and hadn't the money or support to enable me to do this.'

Just prior to their return, the sisters at La Chaumière arranged a farewell concert at Moseley Hall to which they invited everyone who had assisted them during the war, including Councillor John Norbury, who had organised Christmas parties for the children at his home every year. Councillor Norbury's son Joe recalls:

> My parents invited the Guernsey children and staff to our home that very first Christmas, and every Christmas after that. They asked if they should bring their own dishes, but we told them that they were not to be using everyday plates for our Christmas party and we used our best plates. The children enjoyed sandwiches, cakes, jelly, fruit salad and trifle, it was clearly a great treat for them. Then they recited songs and poems, and we played games such as 'pass the parcel'.

At their farewell concert, the Guernsey children sang a song which had been composed by one of the La Chaumière sisters:

Return to Guernsey
The hour has come our Isle is free,
The Long dark night is past,
O' Lord of Hosts all thanks to Thee.
Our homes in sight at Last.
Oh! we shall see our shore once more,
Our lovely Isle of flowers,
St Peter Port is ours,
When back in their loved Island home
The exiles still shall pray,
And think of you, where'er they roam,
That peace may with you stay!
O' England, with the open hand,
To all in want and woe,
God keep your green and smiling land,
Forever from the foe!

When Paulette returned to Guernsey on 26 July 1945, she discovered that her grandmother had died during the war. She was sent to live with an uncle who she did not know at all, and she never saw her father or sister again. In December

La Chaumière School outside Moseley Hall.

2010, Paulette's life was the subject of a BBC documentary, and she was taken back to Moseley Hall to talk about her wartime memories:

> It was wonderful to be able to go back to look at all the rooms that I remembered so well. The people who own it now showed us around and they had a huge book containing wartime photographs. It brought back some really good memories to see the place that was my home for five years.

THE CANADIAN CHANNEL ISLANDERS' SOCIETIES

When news of the Channel Islands evacuation and occupation reached the 500 Channel Islanders living in Vancouver, Canada, a sense of shock swept through the community. They quickly realised that the evacuees would need clothing, shoes, money and medical supplies, and a writer, Philippe William Luce, formed the Vancouver Channel Islanders Society. The society noted at a meeting:

> Thousands of old folks, women and children urgently need help, and every dollar counts. It costs about $1,000 a week for shoe repairs and dental attention alone. Every letter from the kiddies to their parents in the Islands costs one shilling and families building homes in England need stoves, furniture, bedding, etc.

The society's newsletters give details of the fundraising efforts they made. They sold Christmas cards and Jersey seed potatoes, and held raffles – with one prize being a prize Jersey calf which raised $3,000.[3] Local people donated clothing, shoes, socks, quilts and books to the society, which were sent to Victory Hall, 535 Homer Street, Vancouver, for packaging on Thursday afternoons. The society organised lunches for which admission was $25 per person, together with musical evenings, concerts, film shows and picnics. In October 1941 the Vancouver Lions Club donated all the proceeds of its annual charity concert to the society, which featured an appearance by Lansing Hatfield, a star of the New York Opera. By February 1942, the Vancouver society had sent $3,254 to London for the evacuees together with 119 crates of clothing, and letters of thanks began to arrive from Channel Island evacuees in England – 'More and more letters of thanks are coming from the recipients; some exceedingly touching scribblings from little children.'

Some of the Canadians who donated clothing to the society placed little notes in the pockets of coats and jackets. A Guernsey boy at the Forest School in Cheadle Hulme, Cheshire, found the following note in the pocket of his coat:

Note from Canada.

To the little boy who receives this parcel. Please write to me at the above address and let me know how you like it. May God Bless you, and keep you safe from harm. Sincerely yours, Mrs C.J. Collett.

Another society was established in Victoria, Vancouver Island, containing around 100 members. At their first meeting in August 1941, the committee decided to arrange a Channel Islands Arts and Crafts event, to arouse interest in the islands, and between 1941 and 1945 the Victoria society raised $4,992 for the evacuees. They used the Women's Institute rooms on Fort Street for the collection and packaging of clothing, before sending the crates to the Vancouver society, or directly to London.[4] It is not known exactly how many more Channel Islanders in Canada carried out this wonderful work, but their efforts clearly went a long way in helping unfortunate Channel Islanders in England who had been torn from their homes.

MR JOHN W. FLETCHER

One elderly man in Lancashire outdid the fundraising efforts of most individuals in the communities into which the Guernsey evacuees arrived. In 1940, seventy-two-year-old Mr John W. Fletcher was a retired commercial traveller, and had been a director of the Casket Confectionery Company. His grandson, Ron Standring, remembers the arrival of the Channel Island children in Bury in Summer 1940:

My Grandpa Fletcher not only felt a great sympathy for these kiddies, but wanted to do something to help them. When the evacuees arrived, he naturally responded, particularly as he realised that the evacuee children would not receive any Christmas presents from their families who were in the occupied Channel Islands. He had been a commercial traveller, and had travelled all over the world, crossed the Atlantic, and made contacts wherever he went. So he contacted these people and told them what he was intending to do, to raise funds to give them presents – and asking for their help. It came in waves, willingly.

John Fletcher explained why he had begun his fundraising efforts in 1940:

I wondered, what could I do for the coming Christmas to help to brighten and cheer these children's lives on their first Christmas in a strange land? I sat down at my desk and got busy. I wrote letters and sent them out to some hundreds of friends, mainly to old time pals of mine in the United States and Canada whom I had visited in their homes since I retired from the business. Also to others in Australia and New Zealand.

In December 1940 he arranged a Christmas party at which, dressed as Father Christmas, he presented 200 of the Channel Island children with gift parcels. His main focus was on the orphans in the Guernsey Children's Home who had been evacuated to a large house in Bury, 'Danesmoor', under the supervision of the master and matron, Mr and Mrs Brown. Sheila Laine's mother worked at Danesmoor during the war, and Sheila recalled, 'He was always warm and welcoming, and I believe the Danesmoor children called him "Uncle Fletcher".'

Mr J.W. Fletcher.

Postcard sent by Mr J.W. Fletcher.

In 1941, John Fletcher approached friends and colleagues again, by sending them an appeal postcard. One side featured a photograph of the staff and children of the Guernsey Orphanage, while the other side thanked the donor for their cheque of Christmas 1940. It also hinted at another donation for Christmas 1941, with John Fletcher stating:

> Believe me, the whole of these 200 unfortunate little ones got a great thrill on Christmas morning 1940 when on awakening, they found their gift parcel at the foot of their bed or cot. I am hoping to be again able to buck them up this year.

Throughout the war, John Fletcher continued to collect cash donations from friends and colleagues, purchasing at least 300 Christmas parcels every year. He also placed appeal letters in newspapers, and he received this letter from a young couple in Cheshire:

> Please accept this enclosed gift of five pounds towards your Children's Fund. We send it as an offering of thanks to Almighty God for the safety and preservation of our own two little daughters.

From 1943 he raised enough money to buy presents for the evacuee children who were living in the Tottington area, close to Bury, and parents and billeters were notified of this by the local billeting officer.[5] Margaret Cornick remembers attending these parties, at which the children were given their presents. If there were any funds left over, John Fletcher took the evacuees for day trips, and Derek Dorey recalled, 'Mr Fletcher used to visit us, and take us out, and sometimes he would give us little bags of sweets or an orange.' It was not just the Channel Island children that John Fletcher cared about. Sheila Laine's grandparents lived on Bury's Chesham Fold Estate with many other evacuee families, and John Fletcher regularly visited her family to see how they were managing.

In 1944, encouraged by the success of the D-Day invasion, John Fletcher produced a 'Channel Islands Victory Souvenir' booklet. He had clearly been caught up in the evacuees' optimism that they would soon be able to return home, although this would not actually take place until the summer of 1945. The booklet was sent to those who had donated money for Christmas presents and was also given to some of the Channel Islanders. It thanked everyone who had supported his fundraising efforts and asked for one final donation to be submitted to cover the cost of purchasing savings certificates for the children:

> It will be a wise and helpful procedure to send every one of these bonnie lads and lassies back to their Island homes, with a small nest egg of savings.

The booklet also contained a message that had been received from Buckingham Palace:

> Princess Elizabeth and Princess Margaret send best New Year Wishes to the children from the Channel Islands and hope they will have a happy party.

Also included were letters written by some of the Guernsey orphans, 'Thank you once again for all your kindness to us,' 'I am writing to thank you for all the outings you gave us . . . also for the parcels that I greatly treasured.' Mr Brown, the master of Danesmoor, also included a letter of thanks:

> On behalf of the children under my care at Danesmoor, I would like to thank you and all those who have so generously given donations, thereby making it possible for every child to have a Christmas parcel during each of the four years we have been in the Mother Country. I have no need to tell you how much these children have looked forward to the parcels.

Victory souvenir.

In December 1944 when Mr Fletcher presented 300 savings certificates to Channel Island children, he was surprised to receive a gift himself. The orphanage children presented him with a book, *Lancashire Idylls*, which contained some of their signatures. It was accompanied by a poem that had been written for Mr Fletcher by Guernsey evacuee Irene Guille:

We the Channel Island evacuees present to you this book,
You'll find inside each youngster's name whenever you should look,
We hope you will accept it as a gift of love and joy,
For you have been a Santa Claus to every girl and boy.

Four Christmases have come and gone since we came to Bury town,
And each time you've sent us parcels. No child has been let down,
So we thought when we have to leave dear friend we'd like to give this
    little gift to you
With the best of Christmas wishes and greetings warm and true.

So when we have to leave dear friend to sail home across the sea.
You'll have something to remind you of your little refugees.[6]

In May 1945 John Fletcher shared the evacuees' joy on hearing the news that the Channel Islands had been liberated from German occupation. He also received a donation and letter from one of his supporters, Henry J. Allen, ex-Governor of Kansas:

I send my sincere congratulations upon the occasion of your Victory Farewell Tea Parties. My thoughts and my prayers will be with the children and you when the time of parting comes. May God bless you all now and always.[7]

In July around 400 children and parents attended John Fletcher's farewell party at the Co-operative Society Café.[8] David Kreckeler remembers it well:

We were all sitting at long tables and when the individual plates of food were brought out, they ran out just before they reached me. When the next lot came out, they started with the person on my right, missing me out again! I eventually got a plate though!

At the party, John Fletcher told the children:

Little did any of us think in the year 1940 when you came over here to dwell in our midst, that more than five years would come and go before you would

Mr Fletcher in Guernsey after the war.

be able to travel back to your sunny Islands . . . May God's richest blessings be yours and nothing but good come to you and your loved ones in the days that lie ahead. If I am spared I am living in the hope of some day visiting your bonnie Homeland across the sea and meeting you all again, face to face.[9]

John Fletcher was granted his wish to see the evacuees after the war. He visited the island every other year on Liberation Day, but in July 1950 he attended a concert evening at the Ebenezer Methodist Church Schoolroom and was reunited with many of the youngsters whom he had not seen since 1945:

> Some of them had changed beyond recognition in the few years since their departure from the North Country . . . they recognised Mr Fletcher immediately – once seen never forgotten!

He was presented with a traditional Guernsey milk can as a token of their regard, and photographed with some of the evacuees. He visited the island again in 1951, and presented some of the children with a signed book, *The Last Wolf*, and Sheila Whipp still possesses her copy which means a great deal to her. John Fletcher passed away in February 1953, but is still fondly remembered by all the evacuees who knew him. In September 2010, a public appeal for memories of his kindness met with an amazing response from the people of Guernsey. Barbara Mechem recalled that 'the only Christmas presents I received during the whole of the war were given to me by Mr Fletcher.'

NOTES

1   Interview with Paulette Tapp, December 2010, p. 2.
2   FDR Presidential Library, FPP Archives, Paulette Le Mescam biography sheet, February 1943.
3   Martel, Diary, Vancouver Channel Islanders Society Minutes, 20 March 1942.
4   *The Daily Colonist*, Channel Islanders in Victoria, 3 May 1979, p. 4.
5   Bury Archives, Channel Island evacuee files, Memo from Tottington UDC, December 1943.
6   Guille and Whipp family papers, poem written by Irene Guille.
7   *Bury Times*, August 1945, Our Farewell to Channel Island Refugees – see also http://www.kshs.org/kansapedia/henry-j-allen-guernsey-evacuees/17600.
8   *Bury Times*, 1 August 1945.
9   L. Torode family papers, speech by J.W. Fletcher for Channel Islanders farewell party, July 1945.

5

THE GUERNSEY SCHOOLS

Before we left Guernsey, we promised the children's parents that
we would do all in our power – morally, socially as well as educationally,
for their children. Now that the Nazis are in control of our home,
that promise becomes more binding.[1]

During the war, many Guernsey child evacuees attended their local town or village school. However, a number of the evacuated Guernsey headteachers wanted to care for and educate their pupils until they could return them safely to their parents in Guernsey. They met with local officials to request permission to re-establish their schools and colleges in England, but not all were successful.[2] Records are incomplete, but in 1944 around twenty Channel Island schools and colleges, containing over 1,000 children, were still operating in northern England. Some school staff wrote diaries and log books which describe their experiences within these unique schools. Some contain copies of letters that were written and received during the war, together with press reports, photographs, and other wartime souvenirs. They show the amount of responsibility that the Guernsey staff took upon their shoulders. They not only educated the children, but monitored their living arrangements, looked after their health, ensured that they had access to food and clothing, monitored their behaviour within the school and the local community, provided comfort in times of distress and guided their employment choices. It would be impossible to record the experience of every evacuated Guernsey school and college within the pages of this book, and more information about Channel

Island children's education in England can be found on my website, and in Brian Ahier Read's book *No Cause for Panic*.[3] I will use the diaries of a headmaster and two teacher's helpers to piece together the story of just one of these evacuated schools – the Forest School.

Percy Martel was headmaster of the Forest School and he kept a diary throughout the entire war. On 21 June 1940, Percy left Guernsey with 134 children, 4 Guernsey teachers and 14 helpers – Guernsey women who each took charge of a group of children. Two of these helpers were Mrs Reta Batiste and Miss Muriel Parsons, who also wrote wartime diaries. Muriel Parsons was twenty-eight years old when her sister, Beryl, rang Muriel to say, 'Our school has been booked for tomorrow's boat, I need a helper for my class, will you come with us?'[4] Muriel agreed to leave with the Forest School, while her parents said they would leave the following day. Muriel packed some clothes but could not take the stuffed koala bear that she had owned for years, and wrote later:

> Grown up as I was, I can remember the unreasonable sadness I felt at having to leave him at home . . . but he was too big and would have taken up too much space in my one valuable piece of luggage. I managed, however, to find room for my camera.

Percy Martel's son Derek explained why Percy did not take his own family to England with his school:

> After a long discussion between my parents my mother felt that I was too young at four years old to go to an unknown destination in England. She decided to stay in Guernsey with both sets of my grandparents until my father had found suitable accommodation for us all.

At 9.00 a.m. on 20 June, the Forest School staff, the helpers and 170 children gathered at the Gouffre Hotel, in readiness for evacuation. They chose to meet at the hotel rather than on the school premises because the Forest School was very close to the airfield. Percy noted that one of his teachers had become too hysterical to evacuate with the school, and failed to report for duty, and he later wrote 'she had already left the island, without leave, by mailboat.' Muriel Parsons described how Percy formed the school into groups consisting of twelve children to one teacher or helper:

> The helpers were given a sash made from an arm sling, and this they wore over one shoulder . . . each sash had a number on it. The children had only to remember their group number. A good idea as some of the helpers were strangers to the children.

In common with several other schools, the Forest School discovered that no evacuation ship was available to them that morning. The group dispersed then reassembled at 1.00 p.m., then again at 5.00 p.m. and once again at 7.00 p.m. As no ship had appeared, Percy sent the children home. The following day, the school reassembled, but only 134 children turned up out of the previous 170. Percy believed that this was due to the inconvenience caused by the delays on the previous day, and a rumour circulating the island that the situation in Guernsey was not as serious as it was painted.

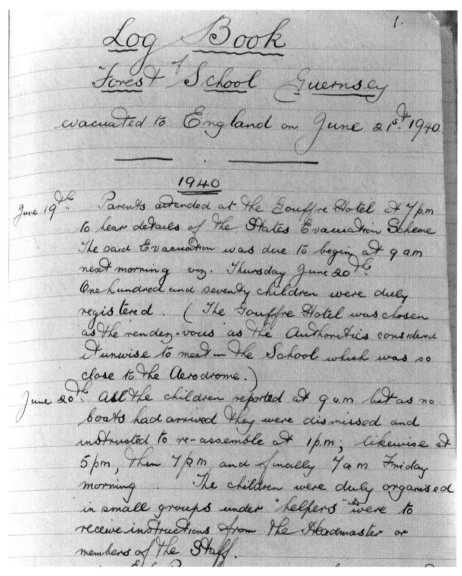

The first page of Percy Martel's diary.

At 9.00 a.m., the Forest School group boarded the SS *Viking* together with staff and pupils from several other Guernsey schools. The ship left Guernsey with almost 2,000 on board. It would have sailed earlier but the schools experienced trouble with parents who could not make up their minds at the last moment whether to allow their children to go or not. Captain Harry Kinley described the Channel crossing as follows:

> Because we were a coal burning ship, we were very conspicuous and a passing warship signalled a message: 'You are a pillar of smoke by day and a ball of fire by night and can be seen for twenty miles.' We signalled back: 'Thank you, we know.'

Percy Martel noted that the journey passed without incident. However, in complete contrast, Mrs Reta Batiste wrote:

> There were no lifebelts available for our children . . . if the boat goes down, down we go – we had no convoy at all, it was just a risk. On the way rumours that we were bound for Canada, what a shock again . . . by now all the children were sick – it was the lack of air and they were frightened and homesick.

The *Viking* reached Weymouth at 2.00 p.m., and the evacuated school party was directed towards a large cinema. Once inside, they were taken to the balcony which had been turned into a temporary consulting room. Muriel Parsons described the evacuees' cursory medical examination:

> The medic in charge gave one look at my sun tanned face, took a peep down my throat and asked 'Had any illnesses lately?' I grinned at him, 'Measles, when I was five, is the last I can remember.' He grinned too, 'Pass, Friend,' he said, 'All's well.'

This examination was followed by tea and refreshments in the Winter Gardens. The Forest School group boarded a train at 8.00 p.m., and their travelling companions included two other Guernsey schools, St Martin's and St Joseph's. No one knew their final destination, 'not because we didn't ask but because no one would tell us; it seemed they were not allowed to do so.' Diaries record the evacuees' comments as they saw strange new sights through the windows of the train, 'What funny animals, are they cows?', 'Course they can't be, cows aren't black, they're brown aren't they?' and 'Do all English people live in those dirty little houses?'

Eighteen hours after they had left Guernsey, the train arrived in Stockport, Cheshire at 5.00 a.m. Muriel Parsons was amused to find interpreters waiting on the platform and described a conversation that took place between herself and a male interpreter:

'We understand the children speak French.'
'Well so they do, sometimes, but it's not the French you would know.'
'Do they speak English then?'
'Try them and see.'

The man then spoke to the children, and was surprised to hear them answer him in at least as good English as his own. The Forest School group were taken to the Masonic Guildhall where two large rooms had been filled with 150 camp beds, with 4ft of space between each bed. Percy Martel described conditions there:

We settled down in both large rooms, each helper with her little group. Our bed was our new 'home'; it was bed, chair, table, dining room, wardrobe and the spot where we entertained all our acquaintances and fellow travellers. There was no privacy whatsoever.

Masonic Guildhall, Stockport.

From the moment that the Forest School arrived in Stockport, Percy's diaries describe his meetings with billeting officers, education officers, Ministry of Health officers and welfare officers. Stockport Council arranged for St Thomas' School to organise games for the children, and local boy scouts took the children to a park to play cricket and football.

In addition, people began to arrive at the Masonic Guildhall loaded up with piles of books and toys for the children, and books for the adults. Rose Short also recalls:

> Entertainment was put on for us, all the beds were pushed against the walls, so the centre was clear for the performers to sing and dance. One morning I stood on the steps and there walking down the road was a man leading an elephant. I have often wondered since what he was doing and where he was going.

Several days later, the evacuees were amazed to hear that Stockport citizens had donated hundreds of items of clothing to them. They walked to the town hall and were confronted by trestle tables full of clothes, with dresses and coats on coat hangers. Muriel Parsons described it as being 'as good as going into a shop! The clothes were in good condition and the children were fitted out in a very short time.' Muriel herself received a beautiful navy blue satin dress with a scarlet sash. However, this now meant that the teachers and helpers had to take all the children's dirty travelling clothes to the local laundry and hand scrub them.

The evacuees took short walks around Stockport where the children experienced random acts of kindness. On one occasion, Muriel and twenty-three children were passing an ice cream seller and were approached by an elderly gentleman who asked:

> 'Do any of your young people like ice cream?' to which the children replied 'Yes please, sir!' The gentleman then asked 'How many of you?' to which Muriel replied 'Twenty-three, sir.' The man replied 'Good gracious me!' then turned to the ice cream seller, saying 'Twenty-three ice creams please!'

The evacuees were also given tours of local buildings and they inspected Stockport's huge air raid shelter which had been constructed by tunnelling into sandstone caves that had previously been used by tinsmiths, and for storing beer and wine. The shelter could accommodate thousands of people, and Muriel described it as follows:

> There were passages running in all directions, the walls and roof were arched and fairly high, giving plenty of space for air. Wooden benches were placed end to end on either side of the passages, for the whole length of the walls and

this gave seating accommodation for approximately seven hundred people at a time. There were electric lights . . . and a first aid post . . . we were to dive into this haven many a time.[5]

On 28 June, the evacuees received the crushing news that Guernsey had been bombed by German aircraft. Muriel Parsons wrote:

The voice of the announcer gave out news which brought us despair. He told how enemy planes had swooped over the island dropping bombs, and killing some of the inhabitants with machine-gun fire. We could imagine the utter fear and panic which the Islanders must have experienced – in our mind's eye we saw it all.

The following morning Muriel received a telegram from Guernsey, which read 'All is well, crossing first boat'. Percy Martel sent a telegram to his wife and son, wondering whether they would be able to follow him to England, and on 30 June Percy wrote in his diary, 'The wireless notified all – the Channel Islands had been occupied by the Nazis and all communications cut. Now we were completely cut off and what we all dreaded – has happened.'

Stockport Air Raid shelter. (Courtesy of Stockport Express*)*

In common with the other Guernsey teachers throughout Britain, Percy's staff and helpers spent the next twenty-four hours comforting their distressed pupils. Ruth Crozier had been evacuated to Rochdale and recalled 'our teachers were very kind to us as we grieved over our parents. That day they did all they could to make us laugh, with funny games and jokes.'

Percy Martel was now fully determined to keep his whole group together as a school unit until the time came when they could return to Guernsey. He was in luck, as Mr Stringer, the local Inspector for Education, was a Guernsey man who had been living in England for several years. Mr Stringer advised Percy that his staff and teachers could be kept together as an 'organised school party', and that arrangements were being made to move them to a nearby Cheshire village where accommodation would be found for them all. However, on 3 July things took a turn for the worse when the Stockport authorities began to place the children with local families in error. Later a message arrived from the town hall which stated, 'No more children are to be billeted!' but by this time a third of the children had disappeared. Percy was told that they would be returned to him in a few days time, when the whole school would be moved to the Cheshire village. However, Percy realised that foster families could become very attached to children even in a short space of time, and asked 'Why not recall them immediately, it will save unnecessary trouble later?' He was told, 'Let them have a holiday they deserve it, poor kiddies: life is better in a home than in a rest centre.'

On 6 July, the Stockport families returned the Guernsey children to the Guildhall, and, as Percy had feared, many had already become attached to the children, and bought clothing for them:

> Enraged and annoyed, billeters came begging and imploring us to leave the children with them, saying 'We have completely clothed them, costing pounds, now it is all lost! Why weren't we told before?'

That evening, as the evacuees packed their few belongings in readiness for the journey to the village the following day, Percy and his staff put some of their precious money towards a collection for the Guildhall staff who had been so kind to them. Reta Batiste wrote, 'Mr Martel presented the Manageress, Miss Deneer, with a lovely fruit dish and Nurse Dacre with a fruit plate. They were both taken completely by surprise.'

The following morning, the group travelled to Stockport railway station, where they met up with other groups of Guernsey evacuees being moved to nearby villages. Reporters were waiting to interview them, and because children usually speak their minds, their answers to the reporters questions were brutally honest:

'How do you like our little town?'
'I don't like it much, it's dirty.'
'What else is there that you don't like?'
'There isn't any sea, you've only a pool.'
'You will be going on another train soon do you like trains?'
'Yes I love them! We don't have any you know.'
'Well I am glad we have something that you like!'

After a journey of 4 miles, the group disembarked from the train and were told that they were now in the village of Cheadle Hulme. Teachers' helper Muriel Parsons and her sister Beryl were billeted with a local woman and Muriel recorded her happiness at sleeping in a real bed again. 'It was lovely to have a feather pillow on which to lay my head, and a treat to sleep between cool sheets instead of army blankets.' However, as the schoolchildren began to be chosen by local families, Percy realised that Stockport officials had not communicated clearly with the officials in Cheadle Hulme:

Officials had not been informed that there were mothers with children in our party, so they were not prepared to billet them together. They were split up – one child here, one child there, and the mother elsewhere . . . the scene defies description, we shall never forget it, these mothers had lost their homes, their husbands and everything they possessed, and just clung to their children as their last joy.

Reta Batiste also described the scene:

Everything seemed to go topsy turvy . . . my own children vanished and were billeted out separately . . . I had left my husband behind on Guernsey . . . it was too much for me to bear! I went to find our headmaster and explained to him how I felt. The officials found Bill and Joan and returned them to me that evening . . . an elderly lady had apparently refused to take anyone in earlier that day. She saw me, took pity and said she would have us.

A short time later, Percy was delighted to learn that he had been given permission to re-establish the Forest School in Cheadle Hulme's parish hall. The teachers visited local schools to ask for spare books and equipment, while the helpers and teachers cleaned and scrubbed the hall. Five schools donated text books but they had no school equipment to spare the evacuees. The only downside to having their Guernsey school in the parish hall was that the children had to put away their desks and chairs at the end of every day, because there were private functions, such as weddings, taking place in the hall at evenings and weekends.

*Bill Batiste in
Cheadle Hulme.*

Percy Martel now had to advise those who had come along as helpers with the school that their work was now complete, and unless they had infants, they now had to find employment. Muriel Parsons obtained work at a local bakery, Armitages, on Castle Street, Stockport, although the size of the bakery seemed practically industrial compared with the small shop that she had worked in back in Guernsey.

The health of the children was important to Percy and from the moment that the school opened its doors, he wanted to provide his pupils with hot school dinners. Mary Arrowsmith was the caretaker of the parish hall and she was concerned that the young Guernsey children had to walk between the school and their billets every lunchtime, in all weathers. Mary provided catering for the private functions that took place in the hall and she encouraged Percy in his attempts to provide school dinners for his pupils. Countless letters were exchanged between Percy and the education office, and in February 1941 he received permission to open a school canteen, and was told that Mrs Arrowsmith's wages would be paid by the council. During their first week of school meals, the Guernsey children and teachers enjoyed the following:

Cheadle Hulme Parish Hall.

Monday	Irish stew and rice pudding
Tuesday	Stewed steak, cabbage and potatoes and jam pastry
Wednesday	Soup, boiled sultana pudding and custard
Thursday	Cold meat, potatoes and gravy and sultana pastry
Friday	Hot pot and ground rice pudding and jam

Mary's granddaughter, Wendy, occasionally helped her grandmother in the kitchens and recalls:

> My grandmother made a real fuss of the evacuee children, but if a meal was to be served at 1 p.m., you had to be there on the dot. If you were late, adult or child, she had a word with you! At Christmas she made coloured sponge cakes for the children and teachers, to cheer them up because they were separated from their families in Guernsey, she was a very inventive cook.

By the end of the war, it was calculated that Mary had cooked around 125,000 school meals for the Guernsey staff and pupils.

During the war, the Ministry of Education declared that children evacuated from Guernsey could take a scholarship examination which gave them a chance to progress to the senior Guernsey schools that had been re-established in Britain. When a child was transferred to secondary school, a member of staff escorted that child by train to their new school and billet. However, problems often arose because poor arrangements were made between the two different local authorities. Two girls were escorted to the Guernsey Ladies College in Denbigh, Wales, and Percy wrote in his diary:

Mary Arrowsmith, the staff and children of Forest School.

Although I wired the time of our arrival, no one met the train, the THIRD time out of a possible three that we were left stranded! Miss Nevitt proceeded to the billeting office and was advised that no wire had been received. Arriving at one billet, the lady met them sternly saying, 'Haven't you been informed? I sent a letter to the billeting officer yesterday to say that I am unable to take any evacuees!'

On another occasion, Percy escorted a pupil to her new school in Rochdale and no one was there at all to meet them. He escorted one boy to Guernsey's Elizabeth College, in Great Hucklow, Derbyshire, and after saying goodbye to the boy, Percy wrote in his diary:

I noticed the 'boarding school atmosphere' as compared with the homely billets of Cheadle Hulme. I think billets are better, so many billeters have become perfect mothers to our children. That home life so precious to us all has not been lost.

A few weeks later, the boy had written to Percy, to say how miserable he was:

He stated that the fields and hedges were like Guernsey and made him feel homesick. He pleaded for every assistance to get him out of that 'concentration camp'! I regret receiving such a letter, but I had expected it, as the change was such a violent one.

Not wanting the boy to give up a promising education, Percy wrote to him, explaining that when he himself had gone to college, he had experienced similar feelings, but in the end had thoroughly enjoyed college life. 'I told him that he was a courageous boy, a boy that I am very proud of, a boy I admired and that I knew he would stick at it and win through.'

Percy occasionally had to deal with behavioural problems within his school, and always bore in mind his promise that the school would do all in its power 'morally, socially as well as educationally', for the pupils. Juvenile delinquency increased in England during the early years of the war, but most offences were of a petty nature, and minor offenders were usually cautioned rather than charged by the police. However, the number of young people appearing in court who were classed as 'beyond parental control' and 'in need of care and protection' rose sharply.[6] Percy contacted the education committee about one particular boy's worsening behaviour, stating that the lad was poorly supervised in his billet and should be classified as an unfortunate victim of evacuation:

Percy Martel's travel warrant.

He is very promising, but has gradually deteriorated in personal pride, behaviour and general attainment . . . He has always longed for the sea . . . the training ship *Arethusa* presents a grand opportunity for him. May I earnestly appeal to you to do everything to accept him as soon as possible?

However, before this letter could be answered, the boy was arrested for stealing items worth £6. Still unwilling to give up on him, Percy spoke up for him in court, and managed to obtain a place for him on a YMCA Farm Training Scheme, which would stand the boy in good stead when he returned to Guernsey. Percy told the YMCA, 'I feel that this lad has much promise but firm control is necessary; he requires a lead, rather than be expected to act on his own initiative.'

On another occasion Percy explained why he would no longer allow his older boys to undertake paid work after school. Several had previously done so, but this had resulted in:

Bad behaviour, having too much money and spending it unwisely, no one knows if they are actually at work or on the streets . . . the billeters have no direct control of them . . . should any accidents happen I feel that the Guernsey parents would blame us for allowing the boys to do such work.

One unmarried girl gave birth to a baby, and Percy wrote to the Ministry of Health:

The girl states that she will not part with it. Her mother wishes it to be adopted as soon as possible – her daughter is becoming more and more attached each day . . . the girl is only fifteen and cannot work to maintain it and look after it as well. It appears that adoption would be better for the child's future. Can you proceed with the matter?

When two boys were caught in the act of setting off fire alarms, Percy asked Cheshire Council for their help in keeping the incident from being reported to the Stockport police:

I have interviewed . . . severely all the lads, warning them against any such acts of vandalism . . . they never realised the seriousness of their actions. Might it be possible to keep the matter in Cheadle Hulme? Can a local policeman's warning meet the situation?

Percy felt that the severest form of punishment he could offer was the threat of removing a child from the Guernsey school and the company of his or her

Guernsey friends. One letter, written by Percy and signed by three boys, reads, 'I have now understood that this is my very last chance to remain at this school. Any bad behaviour at any time whatsoever, can mean instant dismissal.'

From the moment that the Forest School group arrived in Cheadle Hulme, local people and voluntary groups helped the evacuees, offering cash donations or gifts such as toys, clothing, books and household goods. Ironically some evacuees received clothing that had actually been sent to England by Guernsey people in early 1940, for refugees from Europe. Percy frequently mentioned the generosity of local people in his diary, 'Cheadle Hulme, where we are billeted, has done extremely well; people have collected approximately £200 for clothing our Channel Island children – a really noble and praiseworthy effort.'

Percy placed this newspaper cutting in his diary, adding a handwritten note, 'very true, we are extremely grateful for all the help that we have received':

Lancashire people who go to the Channel Islands after the war with the intention of settling there and earning their living will be helped by the Islanders who are at present living in Lancashire. Others will receive an official welcome. We are anxious to repay the kindness we have been shown here.

After a few weeks in England, the Channel Islands Refugees Committee in London (CIRC) realised that local councils were struggling to find clothing for Guernsey evacuees, particularly because the cost of clothing had risen by 30 per cent between September 1939 and April 1940. Percy was told that he should obtain clothing through both the WRVS and local fundraising activities. The WRVS organised a whist drive which raised £55, and a bring and buy sale at Abney Hall which raised £52. The WRVS were frequently mentioned in Percy's diary, as they found empty houses for the Guernsey mothers to live in, and contributed to the school's fundraising efforts. 'The work done and the sympathy extended to us by the numerous WRVS helpers was indeed marvellous. As our troubles increased, their kindness and sympathetic support seemed to attain greater heights.'

Percy's relationship with the ladies of the Cheadle Hulme WRVS was so harmonious that, on one occasion, he wrote a 'thank you letter' to the Canadian Red Cross for clothing which he had never received, 'The children had not actually received any clothing from this source (others in Stockport did though!) but it was not the fault of the Red Cross. We sent thanks, hoping that this would actually mean clothing for us next winter.'

The school showed their appreciation to the local community by putting on Christmas concerts. Over a two-day period, the children put on several plays, recited poems, and sang songs, ending each concert with the familiar 'Sarnia Cherie'.

As winter 1940 approached, Percy was very concerned about the lack of warm clothing possessed by his pupils, as many were still wearing summer clothing. The situation came to a head when the children were forced to huddle inside the cold, damp school air raid shelter for hours on end. After one lengthy air raid, Percy wrote, 'To the shelters . . . a wet, slippery, muddy lake . . . the roof leaking. To take children from a warm school to such an atmosphere is scandalous, and with, as yet, no winter clothes!'

When Manchester suffered heavy bombing during its own 'blitz', Percy wrote in his diary, 'by the light of the fires burning in Manchester 8 miles away a newspaper could be read in my street! Twelve hours of destruction and terror.' The CIRC asked Percy to visit the Manchester head office of the WRVS to buy winter clothing with the funds that had been raised in Cheadle Hulme. At the time, the WRVS had 1,500 clothes depots in England, which met the needs of evacuees, refugees and homeless people, and much of this clothing was donated by the American and Canadian Red Cross. Percy paid a visit to the 'upper class secretary' of the Manchester WRVS, advising her that he had £200 in cash, that his pupils had left Guernsey wearing summer clothing, and that they had no coats, woollens or boots for the cold weather. He described this meeting as follows:

Although I was forewarned by a friend to the likely reception, such treatment as was meted out was hardly expected. The conversation developed in such a line that it became insulting and rather personal.

He contacted the CIRC to complain that the Manchester WRVS had no understanding of the unique situation faced by Channel Island children:

I regret that I had very little, if any, satisfaction as regards 'Speed' in supplying the heavy clothing we require . . . people have collected approximately £200 for clothing our Channel Island children . . . and will naturally be expecting to see our children benefiting by their efforts NOW.

This friction between Channel Islanders and the upper levels of the WRVS was replicated elsewhere. In June 1941 a rather tense meeting took place in London between the CIRC, government officials, and Lady Reading, who was the head of the WRVS.[7] For some reason Lady Reading took an instant dislike to the director of the CIRC, Mr Weatherall, and a CIRC report stated later:

Lady Reading had shown herself strongly averse to our refugees being given grants of American clothing, which she said would produce a bad effect in America. We had seen the American Red Cross and Minister of Health and were glad to say that neither of them had shared her view.

Within a month, the WRVS in London advised the CIRC that they were no longer able to cope with clothing Channel Islanders, and the CIRC committee advised evacuees that it would now take total responsibility for clothing all Channel Island evacuees.

Channel Island evacuees did not just 'take' from the local community but contributed towards fundraising schemes for the war effort. The Guernsey schools also played their part, and Percy's staff and pupils contributed towards the Overseas League Tobacco Fund which supplied cigarettes to the forces. The children received a 'thank you' postcard from a Channel Islands serviceman called Bill Bradley. In May 1941, the Forest School staff were invited to join a procession of 'Officials and War Workers' during War Weapons Week, which Percy described as 'a good testament to the good work that is being done by this section of the War Machine!' He proudly wrote in his diary, 'The total raised by the people of Cheadle and Gatley, including the efforts of we evacuees, was £270,000, surpassing the original £125,000 aimed for to buy 8 tanks!'

As a raffle prize for War Comforts Week, Percy contributed six pounds of tomatoes which his pupils had grown themselves:

> Our tomatoes were decorated with crêpe paper, ferns and 'Victory Vs' and exhibited on a special table in the centre of the hall with a special notice: Special Gift of the Channel Island Children, Raffle prize – tickets threepence. Over £6 was raised on the day and it was good to give something back to those who have helped us since our arrival in this village.

However, Percy's diary recorded some friction at one fundraising event. A dance was organised at the King's Hall, and the profits were being donated to the Forest School's Evacuee Clothing Fund. Percy wrote in his diary, 'During the evening of the dance, I found out that several people had apparently remarked that such a sum should have swelled the War Weapons fund, rather than being given to evacuees.'

Wanting to subtly remind people at the dance that Guernsey was actually occupied by German troops, he wrote later, 'I stood on stage that evening and said I appreciated the fact that funds had been raised this evening to help those who had suffered as a result of the use of "War Weapons".'

The local families – the foster parents – who took Percy's pupils into their homes became an important part of the children's lives. The first task Percy and his staff undertook when arriving in Cheadle Hulme was to visit every child's new home, not just to inspect their billet, but to form a relationship with the family living there. Percy wrote, 'It was a pleasure to visit them, and to encounter such a friendly atmosphere. Most children seem to be billeted in good homes and quite happy and comfortable.'

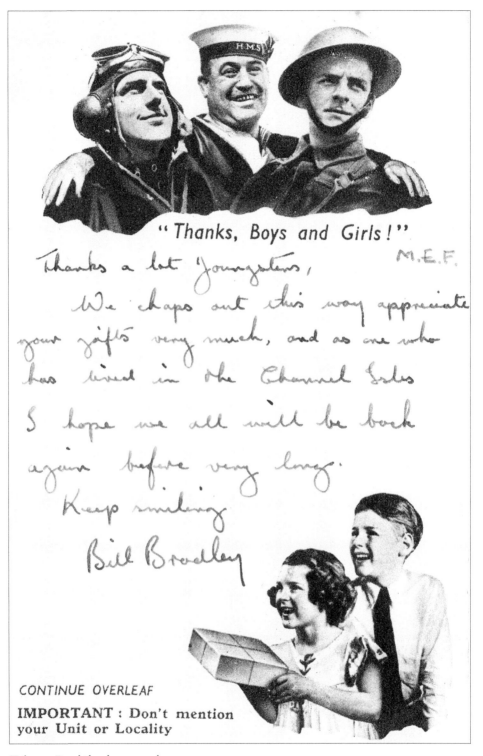

"Thanks, Boys and Girls!"

M.E.F.

Thanks a lot Youngsters,
    We chaps out this way appreciate your gifts very much, and as one who has lived in the Channel Isles I hope we all will be back again before very long.
    Keep smiling
        Bill Bradley

CONTINUE OVERLEAF

IMPORTANT : Don't mention your Unit or Locality

Tobacco Fund thank you card.

*War Weapons Week
programme.*

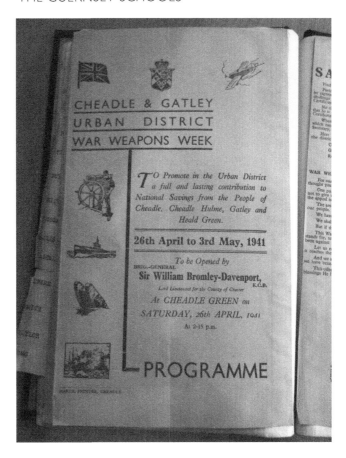

Percy appreciated the efforts made by these foster families, who received billeting allowances for the children, but these sums did not always cover the costs of all necessary food, clothing or footwear. Len Robilliard was happily placed with the Smith family on Ravenoak Road, while his brother and sister lived with other families on the same road.

When children obtained scholarships and moved to new areas, or left school to commence work, Percy encouraged them to maintain contact with their Cheadle Hulme foster parents. In March 1945, one of his pupils, who was now at school in Oldham, wrote to Percy, to ask if she could visit her aunt and uncle at Easter, rather than visiting her foster parents in Cheadle Hulme. Percy advised her:

> You know you promised Mr and Mrs 'S' to spend Easter with them and they are longing for your visit, they have made all arrangements and are disappointed that you were going elsewhere. After over 4 years with Uncle and Auntie 'S' you owe them every holiday – when you return to Guernsey you will see all your relatives, but not Mr and Mrs 'S'.

He wrote to one foster family, saying:

> May I take this opportunity to thank you most sincerely for all that you did for Joan? She was very happy with you and under all your care and kindness, she progressed in every way. I feel that the scholarship she has won will serve her in good stead, but without that I would have been exceedingly happy and content to leave her in your charge for the duration, knowing full well that she could not have been in a better home. I sincerely hope that she will continue to communicate with you from time to time.

On another occasion he noted:

> Mrs 'S' and Mrs 'H' brought their boys into school, and both were very moved by the thought of seeing them journey on. They have done all that they could, their only regrets on seeing them leave was that they were not journeying home to Guernsey.

However, Percy never forgot the children's own parents who were in Guernsey and longing for news of their children. Whenever he could afford to, he sent Red Cross messages to Guernsey. Some went directly to the pupils' family, and one was sent to Mr Le Poidevin to assure him that his sons Harold and Clarence were well cared for. Others were sent to Rector Finey, and one dated May 1941 reads, 'Tell Parents scholars well billeted, clothed, safe, well'. The rector was able to reassure a number of Guernsey's parents that Percy Martel was taking good care of their precious children.

In chapter three we saw the evacuees' efforts to recreate a 'Guernsey community' in England, and the Forest School was no exception. In March 1941 Percy and his staff and pupils paid a visit to Mr Brelsford and his Guernsey pupils in the Cheshire village of Disley. The children played together and had a picnic in Lyme Park, while Percy spent much of the day speaking to the teachers and children to discover how they were coping. Percy's diaries contain details of the Channel Islanders who visited his school, boosting the morale of the teachers and children, and giving them another link to the island that they had left behind. In addition, comforting news of home was usually exchanged.[8] Mrs Merrien of La Chaumière School visited Cheadle Hulme, and Percy wrote, 'She paid us a visit, and the children, as well as ourselves, were delighted to get another "touch" with home.'

The school received a real boost towards the end of the war when the BBC organised a special broadcast from the Forest School as part of its *Sunday Half Hour* programme. Throughout the war, the BBC had been bombarded with requests from Guernsey evacuees for broadcasts to be made to the Channel

Percy's Red Cross letter to Mr Le Poidevin.

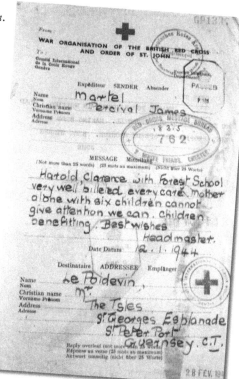

*Evacuees waiting at Stockport
station for a train to Disley.*

145

Parish Hall,
Cheadle Hulme.
16th. April 1945

Dear Mr. & Mrs.

The B.B.C. has been approached with a view to a "S u n d a y H a l f-h o u r" programme to be broadcast from the Methodist Church, Cheadle Hulme.

The singing of Hymns by a united gathering of Cheadle Hulme residents, Guernsey Evacuees, and the billetors, would give expression to the 'goodwill and comradeship' that exists here; the knowledge of which would give the greatest satisfaction to all Channel Islanders wherever they may be - especially those in the Islands and in the Forces. At the same time Cheadle Hulme would establish a link with its own 'Serving Men' and give them much pleasure.

Arrangements have been made for an 'Audition' on Sunday April 29th. at the Methodist Church at 7-45 (following the Evening Service).

Shonld the results be favourable, final arrangements for the actual recording will be made.

Kindly reply by Friday April 29th. if you hope to attend.

Best Wishes and thanks.

Yours sincere'y,

F.J. Martel.

Headmaster

BBC audition leaflet, Forest School.

Islands. Several had taken place, including one by the Girls Intermediate School in Rochdale who sang 'Sarnia Cherie' on *Children's Hour*.[9] However, on many occasions, the government had refused to allow broadcasts because it feared 'that a direct radio message might cause the Nazis to prohibit the use of wireless sets on the Channel Islands.' In early May 1945, the Forest School evacuees and their foster parents sang hymns on the BBC, with the hope that Channel Islanders throughout Britain, in the forces, and those secretly listening to radios on the islands, would hear of the friendship that existed between evacuees and locals in their small Cheshire village.

All of the Guernsey teachers who remained with their evacuated schools carried a burden of responsibility during their five years of exile. Kathleen Cowling believes, 'We were very fortunate in having teachers who stayed with us throughout the war years and provided some continuity in our lives . . . they sacrificed a lot.'

John Davis was evacuated with Elizabeth College:

My memory is of the unfailing kindness of the staff at a time when their own personal lives must have been under great stress, as well as the responsibility of teaching and caring for such a large number of children in very difficult circumstances.

One particular entry in Percy Martel's diary gives an indication of the responsibility he felt for his pupils:

I have acted for the best, no one has been able to guide me. This is where responsibility tells. I have done as I would have done for my own. I have not written so before, but I cannot help stating here that, personally, I should never have left Guernsey last June twelve month. But Duty called, the evacuation was ordered so I left, determined to do all that I could for the children of those who were remaining behind.

NOTES

1   Martel, Diary, 4 October 1940.

2   Read family papers, Notes of Ministry of Health Conference, 29 July 1940; many attendees felt that the Guernsey children should be absorbed by local schools and that the Guernsey teachers should be placed on the register of unemployed teachers.

3   Brian Ahier Read, *No Cause for Panic: Channel Island Refugees, 1940–45*, Seaflower Books, Jersey, 1995. My Guernsey evacuation research website blog is at: http://guernseyevacuees.wordpress.com/evacuation/

4   Island Archive, Guernsey, Muriel Parsons' Diary, June 1940. 'It Happened to Me', p. 5.

5   Island Archive, Guernsey, 'It Happened to Me', p. 21 (The Stockport air raid shelters still exist and are open to the public – see http://www.airraidshelters.org.uk/ (accessible March 2012).

6   Geoffrey Field, 'Perspectives on the Working Class Family in Wartime Britain, 1939–1945', *International Labor and Working Class History*, 38 (Autumn 1990), p. 9.

7   Read family papers, CIRC report of meeting with Lady Reading, June 1941, p. 2.

8   Good news obtained through Red Cross letters was an antidote to the newspaper accounts of Islanders suffering under German Occupation; information about Guernsey was also provided by Islanders who escaped in fishing boats during the occupation, and through letters from Guernsey people who had been deported.

9   *The Intermediate School Magazine*, October 1940.

6

COUNTDOWN TO LIBERATION

D-Day! At last, the day we have all waited for! We went mad of course,
for an hour, but afterwards, I, for one, had a good weep.
What must the home folks in Guernsey feel like?[1]

I n June 1944 the success of the D-Day landings in France gave the evacuees hope that their island would soon be liberated. Some evacuees prepared letters for their families in readiness and Percy Martel wrote one which still remains within the pages of his diary – 'Sincerest greetings and best wishes from the Staff, scholars, mothers and our many friends in Cheadle Hulme. We are proud of your endurance and fortitude, we are all fit and well and longing to see you all again!'

The editor of the Stockport *Review* was equally optimistic. 'News of the invasion of Normandy, after weeks of tension and patient waiting, came as a universal thrill, tempered by some degree of anxiety. To us all it heralds the great day of liberation.'

However, the very success of D-Day meant that food supplies destined for Guernsey were cut off, and both the civilians and the occupiers began to experience slow starvation. Percy Martel's diary contained a Christmas card that had been sold to raise funds for a food relief campaign by the Channel Islands War Relief Association. In December 1944, the *Daily Telegraph* announced that 300,000 emergency Red Cross food parcels were on their way to the starving Channel Islanders:

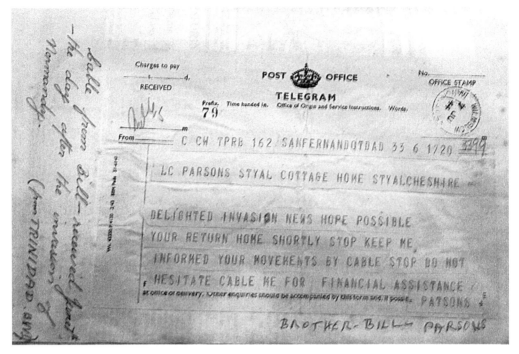

D-Day telegram.

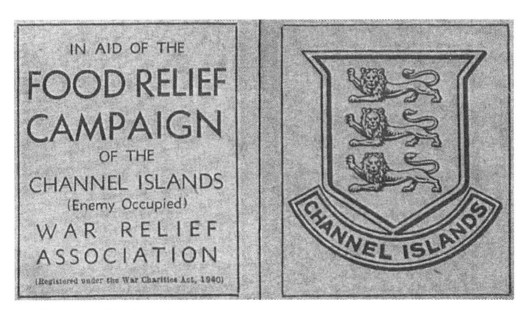

Christmas card for food relief.

The total cost to the British Red Cross and St John organisation of the relief supplied to the Channel Isles on the Swedish ship *Vega* will be £200,000. It is expected that at least two voyages will be necessary for the shipment of the whole cargo.

Confirmation of the delivery of these parcels by the *Vega* gave the evacuees hope that their families would be somewhat relieved of starvation. Two months later Germany contacted the British War Cabinet to propose that 1,000 seriously ill civilians should be evacuated from the Channel Islands to the United Kingdom.[2]

On 8 May 1945, the war in Europe was finally over. The evacuees celebrated Victory in Europe Day with their local communities, but they had as yet to receive news of the liberation of the Channel Islands. Winifred Best recalled the celebrations in Blackpool:

We all went to listen to Churchill's speech, there were crowds by the North Pier, and big loudspeakers up. My sister and I heard his speech, and he said 'Today our dear Channel Islands will be free.' And we went absolutely mad and shouted!

Marie and Mona Martel remember, 'At long last the great day arrived . . . the war (in Europe at any rate) was over and there were great celebrations. A huge street party was arranged for everyone, with food appearing from nowhere on a long line of tables.' Similarly, Rosemary Johnson recalls that, 'We had a big bonfire in our street on VE night, and the kids and dads made figures to burn on the fires, but instead of making a Guy Fawkes, they made a Mussolini and a Hitler!'

Bob Gill was at sea at the time, and recalls:

I can remember standing on the mess deck being told that an important broadcast was coming in, then Winston Churchill came on the radio saying that our dear Channel Islands would be free today. Tears streamed down my face, all my mates didn't mention it until the afternoon, then they said 'We are so pleased!'

Because he was in the navy, Bob managed to make a brief visit to Guernsey within just two weeks of the island's liberation:

The harbour was still full of German craft, German soldiers everywhere. My uncle was sitting on the sea wall, I got out of the car and he nearly fell back onto the beach! I knocked at the back door of my house, nobody came, I shouted (in patois) 'There's somebody at the door!' Father said, 'You can

VE Day party – Muriel Bougourd.

VE Day party – Marie Martel.

wait!' He came out, a marvellous moment. And a lass I had been keen on was there too, plus two little sisters. Because I was in uniform, and the girls had only seen German uniforms, they called me a 'British German'.

On 9 May 1945, a day later than Winston Churchill had hoped, British forces liberated the Channel Islands. The BBC recorded the event as it occurred, and Ted Hamel listened to the broadcast on the radio in Yorkshire:

To us, this was the greatest broadcast ever! It was moving in the extreme and technically perfect. The lapping of the water could be clearly heard as the launch carrying the German commander drew alongside. The BBC did a grand job. We sat there, not knowing whether to laugh or cry.

Raymond Carre was on duty in the fire station when he heard that the Channel Islands had been liberated, 'Hoorah! Hoorah! went up from twenty-five firemen in the room. Such rejoicing.' Percy Martel was so delighted with the news that he wrote a letter to Winston Churchill, enclosing a cigar, and asking Mr Churchill to 'kindly accept it on behalf of all of us.'

Anne Alexandre's family were able to telephone Guernsey later that day and speak to members of their family, after which they organised a big party to celebrate the island's liberation. The Guernsey newspaper featured a poem dedicated to Winston Churchill, and on 7 June, the king and queen visited the newly freed Channel Islands. Ten-year-old evacuee Barbara Ozanne described her joy in a poem which she entered into a children's competition, winning first prize:

> Ring out the bells, Oh London, for Victory is here
> This is no time to be forlorn, but is the time to cheer
> Ring out the bells, Cheadle Hulme,
> For all the Guernsey people will be going home soon.

However, for Gertrude Brehaut, the joy of Liberation Day was overshadowed by the fact that her mother had passed away a few days earlier. Violet Hatton was delighted with the news of liberation, but was still awaiting information about her husband Elijah who was a prisoner of war in Japan.

On 10 May, a group of overjoyed teachers and pupils from the evacuated Guernsey schools took part in a special BBC radio broadcast to the Channel Islands. The honour of reading the opening line of the broadcast fell to Percy Martel:

The Guernsey Evacuee School,
Parish Hall,
Cheadle Hulme,
Cheshire.
11th May 1945.

The Prime Minister,
10 Downing Street,
London.

Dear Mr. Winston Churchill,

As a Channel Islander I write to thank you for all you have done that has led up to the 'Liberation' of the Channel Islands --our 'Island Home'.

I was evacuated to Cheadle Hulme in June 1940 with 150 School children and there had the pleasure to meet one of the villagers whom had spent his honeymoon in 'Guernsey' many years previou and who had brought back a box of cigars as a momento. Unknown to me then, he resolved to keep the last one, and to give it to me when the Islands were liberated:- and true to his resolve he came along yesterday and gave me the cigar.

What a pleasure? and what a gift to an islander?

Will you kindly accept it on behalf of allof us? We regret that it is only 'one', But Guernsey cigars are non-existent and we readily offer all we have or can get.

May the pleasure and enjoyment you so richly deserve and the best wishes of all islanders be yours as you smoke the cigar.

I have the honour to be,

Yours very gratefully,

Headmaster.
Guernsey Evacuee School.
Cheadle Hulme.

Percy Martel's letter to Winston Churchill.

The Hour And The Man

The years have sped and peace
has come,
The way was long and hard:
And through the war-torn
nights and days
Were hearts seared — cities
scarred:
Then, at the crisis of our fate,
A heaven-sent leader rose,
To weld our nation for the fray,
And lead us 'gainst our foes.

He urged, inspired, he toiled
and planned,
He knew our hopes and fears:
Nor held from us our onward
way
Was toil, sweat, blood and tears.
He hurled defiance at the foe
Then at our very gate:
We held our hopes, we kept our
faith,
Nor knew we then our fate.

We heard him speak but in his
tones
Another voice was heard,
That rang through time's vast
corridors
Bade us for battle gird,
'Twas the voice of mighty
Marlboro
That came ringing in our ears:
It gripped our hearts—it steeled
our souls,
And helped to still our fears.

So, heartened for the vital
storm,
Uplifted by his plan:
The days that saw our finest
hour
Gave us our greatest man.
He rallied us, sustained our
Cause,
Our resolution grew:
Five nightmare years we toiled
and strove,
By aid Divine won through.

The hour has passed—our finest
hour.
None shall we know as great:
The man remains, with counsels
wise
To guide our ship of state
To safe and pleasant anchorage
From o'er the troubled sea:
Where we may rest in peace
and live
The glad days still to be!

HAROLD DORNING.

Poem to Winston Churchill.

Sincerest greetings, from all Islanders in the Mother Country, to Victor Carey, Bailiff; Reverend Agnew Giffard, Dean; The States, and all at home. We are proud of you. We acknowledge your courage and fortitude during the long years of captivity with the greatest pride and thankfulness. We now rejoice at your liberation and the prospect of reunion.

In Guernsey, Nora Robilliard had just collected her rations when she noticed a crowd of people by the market steps listening to the broadcast on amplifiers:

I heard the St Peter's School children singing 'Sarnia Cherie'. Then they announced that Mr Le Poidevin from Torteval School, now in Alderley Edge, would speak. Well, it was grand! It lasted for an hour at noon, with others at 6 p.m. and 8 p.m., they were taken in England and specially flown here to be given in town.

MR.MARTELL.   Sincerest greetings from all Islanders in the Mother Country, to

Victor Carey, Bailiff, Reverend Agnew Giffard, Dean, the States,

and all at home.   We are proud of you.   We acknowledge your

courage and fortitude during the long years of captivity with

the greatest pride and thankfulness.   We now rejoice at your

liberation and the prospect of re-union.

(Into Sarnia Cherie - recording by school choir)

We have always longed to speak to you and now the chance has come.

Leaders of the Churches are the first speakers.   Here is the Bishop of

Winchester.

(Bishop of Winchester recording).

BISHOP OF   I assure you that all of you, especially the clergy and the laity of
WINCHESTER.   the Church of England, have been continuously in my own thoughts and
               prayers and I look forward eagerly tocoming among you at the
               earliest possible moment.   It has been with profound respect that we
               have learned of the fortitude and patience with which you have endured
               your trials.   It has been with umility and pride that I have heard
               of the outstandingly fine examples set by many of the clergy in
               your midst.   Problems and difficulties remain.   Reconstruction
               and recovery must take time.

               It will not be possible for all those familiar and personal
               reunions to which you have looked forward to yearningly and so long
               to take place at once.

BBC radio script, May 1945.

This broadcast gave Guernsey parents a real connection with their evacuated children; however, some feared that they would not be able to recognise them when they returned to the island. The *News Chronicle* reported, 'Some mothers are unable to sleep, thinking that they might not be able to pick their children out of the 123 scholars due to arrive with the Vale Primary School.'

In England, the Guernsey teachers had some idea of the difficulties that their pupils might face upon their return home. During the BBC radio transmission, headmaster Frank Le Poidevin had spoken these cautionary words to Guernsey's parents:

> The children have been happy and wonderfully cared for by their foster parents during their stay in Alderley Edge . . . all have grown in wisdom, stature and self reliance. Would be delighted to have photographs of parents as first steps to reunion.

As soon as the postal service between Guernsey and England was reinstated, the head of the Vale School sent photographs of the pupils to their parents in Guernsey. The *News Chronicle* reported, 'some parents have received photographs of their evacuated families, to help them to identify the arrivals.' Headmistress Ida Naftel carefully pointed out to parents in Guernsey that:

> They are reaching out to you but the new ties here are very strong, and this too, is home in a minor sense. To the little ones, five years is half of their lifetimes, and recollections are a bit shadowy. Readjustments there must be, of course, but love and understanding will smooth out all the difficulties.[3]

Thousands of liberation postcards and letters flew back and forth across the Channel and Tony Blampied received one from his Guernsey grandparents, 'Dear Tony, I remember a little fair baby, who did not walk. What is he doing now? How does he like school? Love from Gran and Grandpa.'

Some Guernsey parents wrote to the English families who had been foster parents to their children. Clytha Tourtel's mother wrote to Mr and Mrs Jackson and their daughter Myra, to thank them for caring for her daughter:

> Just a few lines to ask you to accept our heartfelt thanks for the kindness and care you have shown to Clytha. It was a great relief when we had our first Red Cross message to know that she was in a good home . . . we thank you, knowing that we can never repay you, but if ever you are able to travel, perhaps you might care to come to this island for a holiday . . . you are welcome to stay with us as long as you care to.

Guernsey, C.I.

Souvenir of Liberation and Re=Union,

Correspondence to be Written here

May. 8. 1945

Dear Tony

I remember a little fair baby who did not walk, what is he doing now? How does he like school. Love from

Gran & Grandpa

Liberation postcard to Tony Blampied.

Clytha Tourtel and Myra Jackson.

However, sometimes these long-awaited communications contained tragic news. Mrs Ingrouille discovered that her mother had died during the occupation, and Nick Le Poidevin recalled, 'Sadly the first letter that I received from Guernsey told me of my paternal grandfather's death nine days after the liberation.'

Others were told that their homes, places of employment, or family businesses had been destroyed or badly damaged. Mr Reginald Ellis learned that his house had been taken over by German soldiers but that his parents had managed to rescue all of his furniture. In addition, many of the animals in Guernsey had been eaten, so anyone returning to rear livestock realised that they would face hardship. The American Guernsey Cattle Club had anticipated this problem, and had offered to ship Guernsey cattle to the islands to rebuild the herds once the war was over.

In England, the evacuees attended special church services following the liberation of their islands. The Stockport evacuees met at St Mary's Parish Church in the market place, and were joined by the mayor and mayoress, where 'there was a large congregation consisting mostly of women and children and the choir was the Channel Islanders' own.' However, in anticipation of the return home, most of the Channel Island societies disbanded in the weeks following the liberation of the islands. A notice appeared in the Guernsey newspaper to announce the closure of the Bury society, and their secretary, Lawrence Torode stated:

> We have tried to keep the Islanders of Bury united. We have been a great family together of Guernsey and Jersey, and the committee has done great work in providing entertainment besides much welfare work by our women. Much is owed to the Bury people for their support, and when they come to our sunny isles we should give them a great welcome for all they have done for us.

That same month, the Stockport society issued its final *Review* magazine which was simply entitled 'Thank You':

> That the *Review* has been our only link with home has been a popular expression to many readers. We tender heartfelt thanks to our countless supporters. To you all, thank you, and so with full hearts and good wishes, we say Good Bye!

The Portsmouth society endured until 1951, reflecting an indication of its importance to Islanders who had decided to remain in the Portsmouth area.

The logistics of returning thousands of evacuees to Guernsey were complex. Most needed a permit to travel, train transport from northern England to London, overnight accommodation in London, transport to Southampton, and finally, a Channel crossing. Priority also had to be given to those for whom there

Bury Channel Island Society Committee.

was immediate employment, and the idea of holidaymakers visiting the island that year was completely ruled out. On 3 June 1945 the director of the CIRC visited Manchester to address a crowd of 6,000 Channel Islanders at Belle Vue Stadium, stating:

> The immediate return to the islands of a large number of persons would create very serious problems of accommodation and unemployment, and at the outset, provision can only be made for the return of a few hundred persons per week.

He told the crowd that they must apply individually to the London passport office, and if a permit was granted, they could obtain free passage to Guernsey by making an application to their local billeting officer. 70 per cent of the evacuees interviewed for this book said that they always intended to return to the Islands after the war. Stephen de Garis recalls, 'I always understood that we were living in a temporary situation and looking forward to going back to Guernsey.' 30 per cent of the evacuees interviewed for this book decided to remain in England after the war. Some feared that Guernsey would never be the same again after the conflict due to the damage that it had suffered during five years of German occupation. They could also see the benefits of life in post-war England and the new opportunities that were available to their children. Mrs Delaune recalled, 'I was living in a modern house, and I had been in hospital in

Stockport and had been really well cared for. Also the children were very happy here. I decided not to go back to Guernsey.'

Many appreciated the comparatively modern amenities that England could offer, and the wider opportunities for education, healthcare and employment. In 1947, Bury Council noted that eight Guernsey families were still housed in the Chesham Fold Estate where they had been living since June 1940. Yvonne Bristol's father had remained in Guernsey when the rest of his family had evacuated, but after the war, 'he and my mum decided to live in England as they thought it gave us all a better chance. My sister and I were eighteen by then.' The Ministry of Health took note of the large number of young working adults from the Channel Islands who did not want to return home:

> These young people may be eligible for maintenance grants, or billeting allowances may continue for the present. Authorities should arrange for friendly supervision by some appropriate organisation or individual after this boy or girl becomes financially independent; it is undesirable that young people earning relatively high wages should be left without some guidance.

Many evacuees had become engaged or married to local people. Mr E.J. Hamel recalled leaving Bradford station, where:

> . . . there were Guernseymen with Yorkshire wives. Yorkshiremen with Guernsey wives. There were Yorkshire-born children of Guernsey parentage setting off for the new home across the sea . . . and moist eyes at the parting with the many staunch friends we had all made in those memorable years.

Lawson Allez met his future wife, Jean, at the cinema:

> So when the war ended, my own family all went back to Guernsey but I promised Jean that I would return to Manchester. I came back to Manchester three months later and in January 1946 married Jean.

Many of the evacuees who were serving in the forces could not return home in 1945 and had to wait until they were demobbed. Over 200 Guernsey men died in action in the British forces. When John Tippett's father returned home, he decided that his family should remain within the Stockport community in which they had settled and made friends. By then John had joined Stockport Boys Football Club and in 1948 he played in the English Schools' FA Trophy game against Liverpool Boys at Anfield. The first leg was watched by more than 24,000 at Edgeley Park in Stockport, and the second leg drew in 40,000 people. For a town the size of Stockport this was a fantastic achievement, and a

Lawson and Jean Allez on their wedding day.

big day in the history of Edgeley Park and the town. Two of the Guernsey boys who had been evacuated to Oldham played for Oldham Athletic. While at the Guernsey Intermediate School, Sylvester Rabey and Bill Spurdle both played for the school team. Sylvester Rabey went on to join Oldham Athletic, and made five appearances during their 1941/42 season. A press report of his debut game against Bolton Wanderers stated, 'Sylvester Rabey, the Channel Islander, was a centre of attraction. His colleagues from the Grammar School, and his fellow evacuees from Guernsey were there in force.'

Sadly, Sylvester joined the Fleet Air Arm and was killed while training as a pilot in America. Bill Spurdle played football in the navy for several years, then joined Oldham Athletic in March 1948. After making 56 first-team appearances, he joined Manchester City in January 1950. His daughter Kay recalls Bill's memory of his journey to City for each game or training session, 'Dad had to catch a bus from Royton into Manchester, then walk to another bus stop to catch a bus to the training ground or pitch. Then he would have the same journey back at the end of the day!'

*Bill Spurdle at
Oldham Athletic.*

City were relegated at the end of that first season, but Bill was a member of the team which gained promotion back to the First Division in 1950/51. Bill also played in the FA Cup final on 7 May 1955 in front of 100,000 people. After making 160 first-team appearances for City, and scoring 32 goals, he was transferred to Port Vale in 1956 but moved back to Oldham Athletic in June 1957. Bill retired in May 1962 at the age of thirty-six, and in 2005 he was inducted into 'Guernsey's Sporting Heroes', being recognised as one of the most significant sports people produced on the island.

Some evacuees returned to Guernsey just to see family and friends and to inspect the condition of their former homes, before returning to England. Hazel

COUNTDOWN TO LIBERATION

Knowles' father was granted compassionate leave from the army to visit his mother and brothers in Guernsey and Hazel recalled:

> Whilst there he inspected our house which we had all left so hurriedly in 1940, and on his return, he and my mother decided, after a great deal of thought, to stay in Stockport until I had completed my schooling. In the event, father found a job with Manchester Corporation then started his own business in landscape gardening, so we remained in Stockport.

Pamela Blunt's father discovered that the Germans had ruined everything – 'he didn't want to stay there, and came back to England with our dolls and a sewing machine, he later got £50 compensation for losing our home.' Property

Compensation claim letter.

163

Rehabilitation Scheme files in Guernsey's Island Archives show that evacuees spent many months trying to obtain compensation for the loss of their property and belongings during the occupation. Claimants had to list every item that had been within their home on the day that they had evacuated in June 1940, together with the cost of each item. This must have been a very difficult exercise for many people, particularly for those who had decided to make their lives in England. In July 1945, a family returned to Guernsey and applied for compensation because all of their furniture had been removed by German troops. In June 1946 they finally received a loan to enable them to buy furniture for their empty home.[4]

The majority of the Guernsey schoolchildren were scheduled to return to the island in July and August 1945, but their teachers had a great deal of work to

TO THE CHANNEL ISLANDERS – AUGUST 13th, 1945.

Farewell ye children of the Isles,
    We send you home across the sea;
With heavy hearts we see you go,
    And wave good-bye regretfully.

Five years have sped – five growing years,
    Since when you left your Island home
To refuge here.   Do you recall
    That fateful day that saw you come?

So brave you were, so hard you tried
    To raise a smile and check a tear;
Such foreign words were on your tongue,
    We hold it all in memory dear.

Now you have grown from child to youth,
    And we have loved you as you grew;
Think sometimes of your Disley friends,
    When you are in your Isle a-new.

Farewell ye children of the Isles,
    Hold fast the good we tried to give,
And know what else may fade away,
    Your memory will surely live.

Disley poem to the evacuees.

do in preparation. In June 1940 they had merely transported their pupils across the Channel. Now they had to obtain a passport photograph for every child, apply for travel permits and ensure that each child had a medical examination. They also had to prepare lists of items which needed to be packed for the return trip; schoolbooks, sports equipment, clothing, and personal items that had been given to the children by their foster parents. One teacher recalled the packing of numerous school items. 'Gifts of spare text books had been given to us from other schools in Manchester. We of course had arrived here with no books, paper, pens, mathematical instruments etc!'

It was difficult for many evacuees to obtain enough packing cases to accommodate their possessions, and Hodson & Company advised Bury's billeting officer that, 'We have searched the place for suitable cases but the small quantity we have are at present in use, and have been sent out to clients. Should we have any during the next week or two we will let you have one or more.'

Prior to their departure, the Guernsey schools had farewells to make to the people who had helped them during the war in so many different ways. The residents of Disley village were sad to see the children leave, and a poem was written for them just prior to their departure in August 1945. On 21 July 1945, 123 children from the Vale School returned to Guernsey on the *Hantonia*, and the *Guernsey Star* reported their arrival:

> They cheered as the ship berthed, promptly swarmed on to the quay, shouting and cheering and talking loudly in North country accents. Some of them carried puppies and one youngster had a hen and brood of chickens in a cardboard box – a present for his family. Customs officials pounced on him, gravely explaining that it was forbidden to import livestock, and took hen, brood and box into their custody. More than 500 people gathered near the harbour Clock Tower where emotional reunions took place.

Headmaster Percy Martel's diary entries are uncharacteristically sparse after May 1945, perhaps indicating his preoccupation with the Forest School's return to Guernsey. In July 1945, he closed the evacuee clothing fund, and the balance of £40 was sent to Guernsey to be spent on treats for the Forest School children who had remained there during the occupation. On 24 August 1945, Cheadle and Gatley Council organised a civic reception for the Forest School:

> Councillor Grisenthwaite said how pleased the people of Cheadle Hulme were to have been of service to them . . . Headmaster, Mr Martel, expressed the islanders thanks for all that had been done for them during their stay.

Percy also arranged a 'last supper' for the evacuating teachers and helpers. Reta Batiste's diary contains a photograph which shows some of them sitting around a table smiling with delight at their imminent return home. Percy's son Derek recalls:

> My mother and I went to England to meet my father. After five years I only just recognised him. We all returned together on a ship called the *Hantonia*. Because of the mines in the Little Russell we had to sail all the way around Guernsey via the west, south and east coasts to the harbour. When we arrived everyone was amazed at all the amount of barbed wire everywhere.

Back in Guernsey, the school was quickly re-established in its old premises. It was one of the least damaged school properties on the island, having been used as a hospital during the occupation. When the school reopened on 17 September 1945, Percy wrote:

> There were desks but no other furniture; tables, chairs, cupboards, duplicating machines, wireless, typewriter, previous statistics and correspondence, including log books, have disappeared and should be considered 'lost'. The children spent the first day cleaning up, whilst German prisoners took down the barbed wire. 51 children registered.

Forest School 'last supper', August 1945.

In April 1946, as the Guernsey primroses came into bloom, Percy sent 1,000 bunches to Cheadle Hulme as a thank you.

Several adults recorded details of the evacuee schools which returned to Guernsey. Della Mauger wrote:

> Percy and family returned from Oldham on Tuesday morning in charge of 78 children and adults, they spent two nights at a hostel at Waterloo . . . they are delighted to be back in their home and the more so to find it practically as they left it. It is a great joy to feel that the war is really over.

Guernsey teacher Ella Mahy wrote:

> Our departure from Rochdale on August 15th 1945 had its own air of unreality though how different from that of June 20th 1940! As our ship nosed its way into the harbour on yet another perfect morning, on a full high tide, we knew that we had come home to an island even lovelier than some of us had remembered.

Some evacuees wrote letters to the English billeting officers who had been so helpful:

> I am sure you are thinking that I have completely forgotten you. Since we came back three months today – many things have had to be arranged or reorganised, so letter writing was left in the background. You must feel quite lonely without all the turmoil entailed for the repatriation of all evacuees. Once more, many thanks for all your kindness to us all.

When the children returned home, thousands of them had to reconnect with mothers, fathers and siblings that they had not seen for five years and to meet new brothers and sisters that had been born during the war. The situation was different for each family, but was almost certainly influenced by factors such as the age of the child when evacuated, the quality of the relationship between the child and its natural parents, and the quality of the care that had been given to the child by the English foster parents. Many returned to happy lives in Guernsey, glad to be back with their natural parents, and in the island that they loved. A photograph taken of John and David Davison in 1945 captured their joy as they prepared to journey home. Many evacuees settled happily into Guernsey family life although most had to get to know their parents and siblings all over again.

However some children were distressed to leave behind the English 'parents, brothers and sisters' who they had come to love. One English boy recalls that

John and David Davison.

the little Guernsey girl who stayed with them did not want to return to her own parents in Guernsey as she had forgotten them. 'She was dragged kicking and screaming out of our house, which was very upsetting. We did manage to stay in touch, however, through letters.'

Mavis de la Mare was reluctant to leave her foster parents:

I didn't want to stay in Guernsey – my Disley foster parents wanted to adopt me but my parents wouldn't let me go. I remained in contact with Mr and Mrs Mayers for many years and they came to visit me in Guernsey on numerous occasions. I am still in contact with their niece, Pam.

Phyll Board had mixed feelings about leaving her foster family, but then the excitement of seeing her parents took over:

I was going home at last. What I thought was going to be the best time of my life turned out to be quite traumatic. I was a stranger once more and didn't feel part of the family. What a culture shock. It took me a long time to settle down and in fact I did think about going back to Eccles at one stage.

Irene Moss returned home with her four sisters to discover that she now had a brother, and 'as we all entered the house, our new brother hid under the table from these five strange women.'

Win de La Mare recalled:

It wasn't easy, in fact, the truth is, I have never really settled. When I got back home, my mother had two more children, who I didn't know, and I often felt that I just didn't fit in. Also I really missed Ruth, the daughter of the family that had looked after me in Cheshire. She had become a sister to me during the war. We wrote to each other when I got back, which kept me going, and we are still in touch now, and visit each other as often as we can.

Faith Henry lived with the Schofield family in Rochdale:

I have nothing but happy memories of my time there, and had mixed feelings about going home. I became very fond of Mrs Schofield and she was grief stricken when the time came for me to return home. Obviously I had missed my parents but I also felt like a daughter to Mrs Schofield.

When Anne Le Noury returned to Guernsey she was quite nervous about meeting her father. not having seen him for five years:

Mum started waving to people who were laughing and shouting. It was quite bewildering and I was quite wary, when a man came and picked me up and hugged me tightly, but he was nice and cuddly, it was my dad . . . we gradually got used to being together as a family.

Mr Le Conte realised very quickly that his daughter, Margaret, would not remember him when she returned to Guernsey, so he wrote to her in England to introduce himself. 'It will be strange to meet a grown up daughter who left here "a little shrimp". With much love and a speedy reunion, Dad.' Margaret later recalled, 'I remember the arrival, and my mother pointing to my father, "the one with the hat", when virtually all men had hats!' Miss Dorey recalls her first sight of her parents after five years:

They looked thin and worn, not quite as I remembered them, and they had no new clothes at all, mother was wearing my older brother's old school Mac . . .

they collected us in my grandfather's car, which he had hidden throughout the whole of the occupation in a shed covered up with piled up tomato boxes.

Harold Gilbert found it difficult to settle back in with his family. 'Our outlook had changed, we had grown up so it was fairly difficult. At one point, I felt that there was nothing there for me and I wanted to go back to England. But eventually, I got a job and settled down.'

Mollie Rose returned to Guernsey and found it 'a little strange after five years away, almost like living with strangers.' For quite a while, George Gallienne found it difficult to call his mother 'Mum'. Alan Frampton recalled, 'I didn't recognise my father and I asked my mother who that man in the blue coat was.' Another boy recalled, 'I had left Guernsey when I was five years old so when Mum took me back there in 1945, I didn't recognise my dad. We had been apart for so long, we were like strangers. We never formed a proper relationship with each other.'

John Helyer had been evacuated to Bury and had a very difficult homecoming:

First of all, when I was returning, I did not know what my parents looked like, I had no photos. When we met I didn't understand them and they didn't

*John Helyer leaving Bury
in 1945.*

understand me. We had all sorts of problems – it didn't work out like I had expected. And my father died a few months later.

Beryl Merrien had helped to care for the evacuated La Chaumière children for five years, and noted:

Some of our children had been good as gold for five years in Moseley Hall but when they got back to Guernsey they just couldn't settle back in with their families after a five-year gap. And although Moseley Hall kept the children all together, it was bound to be far more institutional than an ordinary billet.

In 2005, Corral A. Smith's study, *The Impact of the Evacuation and the Occupation Experience,* confirmed that many Guernsey family relationships were irretrievably broken down because of the evacuation. A report issued by mental health charity MIND in Guernsey described the far-reaching effects of the evacuation on some children:

The parental separation had a long term effect upon the children, persisting after the reunion with the parents. Of the fourteen children who had problems in adjusting to life on return to Guernsey, eight of these made a satisfactory adjustment after the initial difficulties. So for the population as a whole, the numbers of those who could have been permanently adversely affected by the evacuation could be very large.[5]

What of the thousands of English foster families who had cared for Guernsey children for five years? Of those interviewed for this book, all were happy that the Guernsey children could return home, and promised to stay in touch through letters and visits. However, when the day came for the children to leave, families found it difficult to part with them, particularly parents who had no natural children of their own. One foster mother wrote in her diary:

We had no children of our own, and John had become like our own son. On the day he left, we took him to the railway station to see him off, we were so upset to see him go, but we smiled as we waved good bye as we didn't want to upset him.

Tom Spires recalls sadly waving goodbye when Ces Priaulx left Disley, 'he had become like my own brother during the war, and we were always treated equally.' One foster mother recalled the day that their evacuee, George, left their home:

When we had taken in him years before, I never thought for a minute how hard it would be for us to let him go. We waved goodbye as long as we could and then turned and walked away, neither of us could speak, we were too upset. We went to the pictures. I don't know what we saw but we couldn't go home you see, his little room seemed so empty.

Charles Taylor had been billeted with Mrs Unsworth, in Oldham, prior to joining the army at the age of eighteen. He sent Mrs Unsworth a regular allowance from his army pay, and in 1945 she presented him with a bank book which had £250 in his name in it. Because of her kindness and foresight he was able to use this as a deposit on his own home. George Gallienne remained in touch with his foster parents, Mr and Mrs Bell, until their death, 'I visited them, and they came over here on holidays. I also went to their Silver and Golden Wedding celebrations.' Ces Priaulx remained in touch with the Spires family, and Tom Spires has an

Pam Pillage in 1940.

album of photographs taken of both families since the war. 'We have stayed in touch since, and Ces always sent us flowers at Christmas. He was my best man when I got married in 1960 too.'

Some Guernsey children did not return home to their parents, but remained in England with their foster families. Pamela Pillage's mother could not obtain her own house in Guernsey after the war, so could not provide a home for Pamela. Pamela remained with the Phillips family in Cheshire. 'My time with Mrs Phillips was rather different to being in Guernsey, because at times she was strict, but she taught me love and respect which I am truly grateful for so I consider myself one of the lucky ones.'

Derek Dorey was adopted by Councillor and Mrs Pilling, his Lancashire foster parents:

> I had everything, a better life than I could have had if I went home to Guernsey. I think that's why my mother allowed me to be adopted by them near the end of the war. Sadly the law said that I could not contact my birth family once I had been adopted. I was only young and I hadn't realised that this would be the case. I never saw my mother again.

Richard Smith had left Guernsey when he was only sixteen months old, in the care of his mother's friend. His father, who was stationed in the Isle of Man at the time, found him, and Richard was brought up there by his father's 'lady friend' and her parents:

> I was too young to remember my mother, and I had always been told that she was dead. Years later when I was married, my father, who was rarely in contact, told me that my real mother *was* alive and living in Ellesmere Port! My mother and I met in Chester where I discovered that I now had a sister.

Interviews reveal that many of the evacuees believe they benefited from their experiences in England. Harold Ozanne told his family that, in England, his daughter Joan 'has grown up to be a fine girl and does not need anyone to hold her hand.' Margaret Duquemin noticed differences between evacuees and those who had remained in Guernsey, in attitude, upbringing and conversation. Rose Short agreed, 'it seemed that the evacuees were more independent and had received more freedom whilst growing up in England.' Hazel Hall believes that she gained a great deal from living in England:

> If I hadn't evacuated, I would never have travelled to so many different places, or seen so much. I gained a great deal of experience of life through it.

Ella Mahy acknowledged, 'We had all learned so much in England, not least the value of resilience in the face of change and uncertainty, the warmth of kindness and camaraderie, and the generosity of our Northern friends.'

Guernsey's MIND report noted:

Much of what the study revealed was unexpected to the team, e.g. the freedom found in the U.K., from what was, at the time, a far more isolated community, was beneficial to so many people. For some subjects, the return to the Island was no liberation but a return to a kind of captivity.

Percy and Muriel Rowland's wedding day.

Mr Ninnim's house 'Edgeley'.

Sir Geoffrey Rowland described his parents' reluctant decision to return to Guernsey:

> They had known each other before leaving Guernsey, and were married in Hazel Grove in 1942. They returned to Guernsey with some reluctance in 1945. My mother was always grateful to Miss Morris, who owned the grocery shop, whom she regarded as a lovely employer, and to the customers who had insisted on buying the ingredients for their wedding cake. My dad loved travelling to Maine Road to watch Manchester City, and also to Belle Vue, Manchester, to watch speedway racing.

Frankie Billington believes that his evacuation experience 'was an adventure, providing me with scholastic and artistic opportunities I would never have had in Guernsey.' Len Robilliard became an engineering apprentice, and during his leisure time, he joined the Youth Hostelling Association, cycled for miles, watched speedway racing at Belle Vue and joined the Stockport Sea Cadet Corp. In Alderley Edge, Nick Le Poidevin was introduced to a world of books, plants, art and music. These influences helped to shape his life and Nick won a scholarship to Oxford University, eventually working with the Colonial Agricultural Service in The Gambia.

In recognition of their fond memories of England, a number of evacuees named their Guernsey homes after the places they had known during the war. George Gallienne named his home 'Cloud End' in memory of the happy home he had shared with Mrs Bell in Alderley Edge. Raymond Carre always named his houses 'Kirklees' after the war, while the White family named their Guernsey home 'Heaton Moor'. The Exall family named their home 'Brinnington' while Peter Ninnim's father built a house in Guernsey and named it 'Edgeley'.

Some teenage evacuees were disappointed with their prospects in post-war Guernsey. Irene Moss recalled:

> There was no decent work for young girls in Guernsey after the war! After all that education, and I ended up scrubbing floors! Guernsey seemed so small after the wide roads in England and the wide open spaces of the Cheshire countryside. After 6 months I returned to the English farm where I had been billeted!

Others had to abandon their career aspirations to assist with childcare – Win de la Mare had to care for the younger children in her family. Sheila Whipp was bitterly disappointed with her future prospects:

> I was at grammar school in Lancashire and was looking forward to going to college or university. But in Guernsey my mother was desperately hard up, and

there were no grants in Guernsey, so you had to pay for your tuition fees and it was completely impossible. I felt really hard done to.

Sheila eventually returned to England to study at university as a mature student, then moved into childcare because of her unhappy experience of being passed from billet to billet during the war:

I decided to work with children in care because of my experiences during the war. Kids didn't have any rights then about where they were placed. None of the billeting officers had ever asked me if I was happy, or spoken to me on my own to see if I was OK. I was invisible. My childhood influenced my future and my career.

Beryl Merrien also worked in childcare in post-war Guernsey, due to her experience of living and working at Guernsey's La Chaumière Catholic School in Cheshire:

I had, at first hand, viewed the experiences of many of the children in the school. Yes, there was care from the nuns, and the children were all kept safe, but there was no real 'love' shown to these children during the war. That experience really shaped my life, and I decided that I wanted to work with children in care.

Some young adults found themselves tied to the parental home upon their return to Guernsey. The De Garis family – a mother and six children – had evacuated to England, while Mr De Garis had remained behind to protect their farm. On 26 June 1940, he had written a letter to his evacuated family, his final sentence stated, 'Keep looking up, there will be an end to this one of these days, perhaps sooner than we dare expect, then we shall all be reunited once again.'

Sadly, Mr De Garis died during the occupation, and upon their return to Guernsey, his three eldest sons had to remain at home in order to support their mother in bringing up her younger children. Stephen De Garis recalled, 'The three eldest were adults by then and economically self-sufficient. They took over the role of father at home as much as possible for the youngest three of us.'

As discussed in chapter three, the use of Guernsey patois faded in England during the war. One boy returned to Guernsey and was met by his father who spoke only patois. As they drove home, the only way they could communicate with each other was through smiles and gestures. Joyce Tostevin returned home to meet her grandfather who spoke to her in patois, while he could not understand Joyce's regional accent, making it difficult for them to have a conversation. Stephen De Garis recalled that in his post-war Guernsey school, just a few children spoke patois and they were those who had not been evacuated. In addition, many

Evacuees return to Guernsey. (Carel Toms collection, Guernsey)

Guernsey evacuees now spoke English with distinct regional accents. Ed Renouf recalled, 'It was strange to hear these children speaking in the many and widely varied dialects that they had acquired in their temporary homes.'[6]

One father admitted that his son's voice was like a foreign tongue and he could not understand what he had said because of the accent his boy had acquired over five years. Several were immediately sent to elocution lessons, while Margaret Duquemin recalled, 'I spoke with a definite Yorkshire accent on the day of our arrival. My grandmother was not impressed and straight away sat me down to teach me to speak proper English.'

By November 1945, most of the adult evacuees had returned to Guernsey. Many had said fond farewells to their English friends and promised to write when they had settled in Guernsey. Before she left Brighouse, members of the Methodist Church gave Mrs Doris Rouget a Bible, signed by members of the congregation, as a keepsake.

Of the adults interviewed for this book, 75 per cent returned with their children to Guernsey, and discovered an island that had been torn apart physically, socially and economically. Raymond Carre and his wife Edith returned to discover that their cottage had been demolished, 'to make a rail track in order to convey building materials for fortifications around the coast. All our belongings, furniture, clothing, beds, two new bicycles, radio, etc. had gone.'

Mr Rumens finally decided to keep his family in England as he had a good job, with a detached house and garden, but the family returned briefly to Guernsey to collect their belongings. Before they had left Guernsey they had asked their neighbours to keep an eye on the house for them. They found the house practically intact, containing all their possessions. However, the neighbours asked the Rumens family for payment for this five-year service, and the family had to sell some of their possessions to pay their neighbours. Ron Le Moignan's family were torn over whether to return to Guernsey or not, 'My sister and I and our mum wanted to return, my dad did not. We believe that this issue caused great stress in the family and contributed to the break up of our family!'

Despite the fact that reconstruction work needed to be carried out in Guernsey, evacuated mothers were thankful to be reunited with their husbands after five years apart. Olive Quinn recalled stepping off the boat at St Peter Port, 'My heart was beating 60 to the dozen! Then I saw my husband and we experienced the most lovely feeling of holding each other after five long, weary years.'

Freda Langlois wrote, 'how lovely to set foot on our native soil once again and to be met by those loved ones.' Similarly, Winnie Digard recalled, 'It was a lovely feeling to be back home. When we got off the boat, my husband and my mum and dad couldn't get to me and my children fast enough. What a welcome!'

However, several women returned home to discover that their husbands had formed relationships with other women during the war. One man met his wife and child at the harbour, bluntly advised them of his three-year affair, and said that he did not want his wife or child in his home. A number of mothers found it difficult to adjust to Guernsey life. In England many had worked, made all the decisions and controlled the household finances, but in Guernsey they were expected to return to the role of housekeeper and child minder. In addition, they often had to help to rebuild family relationships. Kath Ozanne returned to Guernsey after five years in Nantwich with her sons, Tony and Michael. In England she had found employment in Boots the Chemists, making lifelong friends with the other employees. Her son Tony recalls:

> Mum enjoyed her new career, giving her a different outlook on life than that of a grower's wife . . . this acceptance of English ways was of little help when they had to yet again uproot themselves to return to island life – thousands of women, like my mother, had to rebuild their homes and re-establish their marriages with husbands they had not seen for years.

Tony also recalls that his father found it difficult to cope with the fact that his boys had spent five years referring only to their mother for advice. 'Whenever

I had a problem or wanted to know something, it was automatic to just say "Mum" and I soon came to know that my father felt excluded and hurt.'

Paul Roget recalled:

Throughout the war, my mum worked, paid all the bills and looked after us kids whilst my dad was in Guernsey. Before the war, she had never worked, so it was all really new to her. It changed her outlook on life and her ideas on what women were actually capable of doing.

Kath Le Poidevin's mother, Cecilia, also found it difficult to adjust:

In Stockport there had been no men in the house, Mum had run the whole show, caring for the children and dealing with money and bills, working at the cinema. So it was a big adjustment for her, back in Guernsey where we had Dad, an uncle and grandfather in the house. There was lots of tension at first.

However, many women were happy to return home to pick up their pre-war roles and to put the war years behind them. Jeanette Le Page recalled her mother's return from England:

Mrs Kath Ozanne with her children.

She just did not want to discuss the evacuation in any way, shape, or form. The stress of the family being separated for five years had told on her. She just wanted to forget about the war and get on with family life.

For five years, the Revd and Mrs Milnes had cared for the Elizabeth College boys in Derbyshire, and their daughter Elizabeth recalls:

My mother was worn out because of the evacuation. She had found it a big strain, being responsible for the safety and welfare of so many other people's children for so long. Back in Guernsey, she had to track down all our furniture, and re-establish the family home. She just wanted to forget about the evacuation and all the responsibility she and my father had taken on, and to look forwards, not backwards.

Some adults returned to Guernsey to discover that their homes were intact, but that many of their possessions had been removed, not just by German forces, but by Guernsey people. The Mauger family's house was completely empty, and a local woman had taken possession of some of their linen and crockery. Weighing up the risk between worsening social relations within her community, and recovering her treasured possessions, Mrs Mauger threatened to involve the police – her linen and crockery were returned to her. This was not an isolated case. Two evacuee families discovered that their furniture had been placed in communal furniture depots and went to claim it. However, families who had remained during the occupation claimed that much of this furniture was theirs, and fierce arguments ensued at the depots.

Among those who shared their experiences for this book, some felt that there was a stigma attached to them in Guernsey because they had evacuated. They felt that they had been perceived as 'cowards', something which Corral A. Smith describes in her Guernsey study as 'emotional segregation'. As mentioned in chapter one, during the evacuation, some officials had tried to dissuade people from leaving the island, and anti-evacuation posters stating 'Don't Be Yellow!' had been displayed. During the war, some Channel Islanders in England had anticipated problems when returning the evacuees to Guernsey after liberation. They felt that there might be animosity towards those who had evacuated from those who had remained behind. They also feared that some evacuees might bear a grudge against officials who had tried to prevent them from leaving in 1940. A confidential memo noted:

The problem of amalgamation of those who stayed and those who went has to be solved. When some time has passed after the re-occupation, passions will have cooled, and the necessity of working together in the re-establishment of everyday life will have restored to the Islands their usual balance and practical good sense.[7]

The memo went on further to say:

There has been much criticism of the circumstances of the evacuation and of the action taken by various officials, much of this may be ill founded, but no judgement must be formed until all the facts are known.

Richard Adey's family experienced distinct antagonism:

My uncle Frank returned to Guernsey in 1945 to his former building firm. He discovered that the only work that an evacuee could get was outside work on roofs. He was told 'take it or leave it. You ran away.' After a couple of years of working outside through some bitter winters, he died from pneumonia.

Jean Dorran recalled:

Each time I started to talk about my evacuation experiences, someone would say 'Well, here, during the occupation it was much worse' . . . so I was effectively frozen out of the conversation – after a time I just shut up and never brought the subject up again. I had quite a hard time during the evacuation, but no one who had remained behind was at all interested.

Some evacuees recall trying to tell Guernsey friends and neighbours about their time in England, and Graeme Symons recalls, 'When we got back you couldn't talk about anything to other people, because they'd just start to talk over you and say, "In the occupation . . .".'

Stephen De Garis recalled that, for years after the war, the occupation was the only theme of most conversations, especially at Christmas. Edna Cave's family never asked her about her five years as an evacuated mother: 'They never talked about it, it was like a closed book to them, they just weren't interested in what I had gone through.

One Guernsey headmaster was criticised for leaving the island. Frank Le Poidevin and his wife had taken the Torteval School pupils to safety in England, and cared for them for five years. In 1945, the children's parents had warmly thanked the couple for all they had done for their children. However, in complete contrast, relations within the Le Poidevin family itself were distinctly cool. Their son Nick recalls:

My parents and I were the only members of our immediate family that had left the island . . . our reception by the rest of the family was not altogether warm. For many years at family gatherings, we were constantly reminded that we had run away from the Germans while the rest of the family had stayed and suffered. In vain would my father remonstrate that he had left out of a sense of duty to the children of his school and their parents. There was animosity, and the closeness that had existed before the war had gone.

Winifred Best recalled, 'Back in Guernsey I met a few people I knew and some looked at me peculiarly because we wore skirts just above the knee in England. To some locals these looked shocking, as if I were on the streets! And of course I was "yellow" too!'

However, as a result of the war work that she had undertaken in the WAAF in England, Winifred had the honour of meeting Princess Elizabeth in 1949 when she visited Guernsey to thank those who had joined the British forces.

Princess Elizabeth chatting to Winifred Best.

Some child evacuees did not talk about their time in England, particularly those whose mothers had remained in Guernsey. Some mothers found it difficult to cope with the emotional attachments that their child had formed in England, and Jenny La Mare recalled:

> My mother did not want to hear me talking about my 'Auntie Maisie' in England, what she did for me, and how much I missed her. I soon stopped talking about my time in Lancashire, as I could see it upset my mum. She felt I couldn't love both her *and* Auntie Maisie – several of my school friends had the same problem, so kept quiet.

However, children like Jenny, who remained in contact with their English billeters, discussed their evacuation memories in letters to England. Guernsey's MIND report noted that in England, 'the good foster mothers gave understanding and love, establishing a bond which still holds.' Win de la Mare frequently discussed her wartime memories in letters to her English foster sister, Ruth Jackson, while Audrey Rose stated, 'From the moment Pam went back to Guernsey, we wrote to each other once a week, and once we started earning our own money, we visited each other as often as we could. Seventy years later, we still write to each other every week!'

Some children also had the chance to discuss their experiences with teachers who had also been evacuees. When their schools reopened in Guernsey in 1945, these same teachers provided a sense of continuity, and understood what their pupils had gone through during the evacuation. Ruth Benoit stated, 'I couldn't talk to my mum about it, but I knew I could talk to my teacher if I wanted to.' Alec Rose, recalled, 'whenever I see one of my form, they can always talk about their experiences to me.' Similarly, Molly Cowley said, 'When we got back to Guernsey, we saw Mr Martel every day and could chat to him about the war, and our time in Cheadle Hulme, and he seemed glad to talk about it too.'

David Marchant remembers, 'The fact that I had evacuated with my teachers and remained in their classes after the war, created a bond between us, which I think helped me cope with the situation at home.'

A number of evacuees believe that, had thousands not been evacuated in June 1940, many people in Guernsey might have died of starvation during the occupation. Irene Moss returned home in 1945 and recalls her mother saying 'if you and your sisters had not been evacuated I just don't know how I would have managed to feed you all!' John Le Page was evacuated with his two sisters, and upon returning to Guernsey in August 1945, his mother told him of her struggles:

I will always remember her words. She told me that there just was not enough food on the island during the war, and during the last year she had found it hard to feed the rest of our large family. She told me 'If you three children had not been evacuated, I just don't know what would have happened to us all. In a way it was a blessing that you left, for I would never have been able to provide food for you all. Some of us would surely have died of starvation.'

Hardly a family on Guernsey was untouched by the German occupation of the island. The evacuated, the occupied and the deported all suffered in their different ways and for many, issues of family separation affected their lives after the war was over. Many who lived through this traumatic period of their island's history have not yet shared their wartime stories. As a result, this book is a contribution to a story that is still evolving.

NOTES

1   Guernsey State Archive, Muriel Parsons' diary, 6 June 1944.
2   War Cabinet Report of 6 February 1945, The National Archives, CAB/66/62/5.
3   'Motherly love away from home', *Guernsey Press* (18 June 2010), p. 25.
4   Island Archive, Guernsey, Property Rehabilitation Scheme files.
5   *The Evacuation from Guernsey – The experience of school children and its effects: a Biographical Study by Guernsey MIND*, 1986, pp. 6–8.
6   *Daily Colonist* (9 May 1939), p. 8.
7   Brian Read Archive, CIRC Memo, 7 July 1943, p. 2.

7

COMMEMORATION OF THE EVACUATION

In Guernsey in May 1946, a Liberation Day Parade gave thanks to the communities on the mainland that had cared for its evacuees, and a photograph taken that day is shown on the front cover of this book. Between 1945 and 1953, Guernsey sent gifts to many of the towns and villages that had cared for the evacuees. Among these were the people of Cheadle and Gatley who received a Guernsey oil painting, while the villagers of Disley received an inscribed copper jug.[1] Every May, around Liberation Day, Disley parish church flies the Guernsey flag in memory of the evacuees who lived in the village for five years. Many of the areas which had received Guernsey evacuees erected their own plaques and memorials. During a visit to Guernsey in the 1950s, Mrs Arrowsmith, who had fed the Forest School children in Cheshire during the war, was presented with an inscribed copper jug.

Many of the evacuees maintained contact with the families who had cared for them, writing letters, sending cards and visiting each other whenever they could afford to do so. One Lancashire family missed their little Guernsey boy so much that they moved to Guernsey to live near to his family. One evacuee, Raymond Carre, travelled to Canada where he visited the Canadian Red Cross. He presented them with the Red Cross quilt that he had been given during the war in Halifax, Yorkshire, together with his grateful thanks.

In 1990, on the fiftieth anniversary of the evacuation, a number of reunions were arranged in Guernsey by the evacuees themselves. That same year, several reunions were arranged in places such as Oldham, Rochdale, and Nantwich, where Guernsey evacuees were reunited with each other, and with members of the English families who had cared for them. On 27 January 2008, a Channel

Islands Evacuees' Service was held at Les Capelles Methodist Church, Guernsey. The service was based on one that had been held at St Martin-in-the-Fields, London, on 31 January 1943.

In September 2009, Mrs Joan Ozanne set in motion plans for a one-day event in Guernsey, to officially mark the evacuation. I provided assistance to Joan from England in order that Guernsey evacuees living on the mainland could attend the Guernsey event. It took place on Saturday 8 May 2010 and was attended by hundreds of evacuees, together with seven English mayors and a number of evacuees who had travelled from the mainland. A civic reception was held in the Bailiff's Chambers, an evacuee's lunch was organised, and a commemorative plaque was unveiled by Guernsey's Bailiff, Sir Geoffrey Rowland, and Mrs Joan Ozanne. I also provided assistance to Guernsey Post on the creation of a set of commemorative stamps to mark the seventieth anniversary of the evacuation. I have regularly spoken to Jim Cathcart on BBC Radio Guernsey about my work, and he has greatly assisted me in contacting former evacuees on the island.

Guernsey events, talks and exhibitions were organised by myself and Stockport Council, Oldham Local Studies, and Bury Archives in 2009 and 2010. In June 2010, I worked with Stockport Council to organise a three-day reunion for Channel Island evacuees. This included a special service at St Mary's Church where many evacuees had worshipped during the war. At the reunion, evacuees living in Guernsey were reunited with Guernsey evacuees living in England. Sir Geoffrey Rowland, the Bailiff of Guernsey, gave an emotional speech in Stockport Town Hall, referring to the kindness of Stockport people towards his own parents in 1940:

In 1945 Islanders left Stockport filled with joy at the prospect of a reunion with their families and friends in Guernsey, but they knew that they had made many friends whom they would never forget, and to whom they owed a debt which they would never be able to repay.

At the Stockport reunion, former child evacuees had the opportunity to meet up with other evacuees, surviving members of the families who had cared for them during the war, and volunteers who had assisted the evacuees in 1940. A blue plaque was unveiled at Stockport railway station, and Stockport's mayor, Councillor Hazel Lees, stated:

This evacuation was a remarkable episode in the long histories of Stockport and the Channel Islands. Strong links were forged between our two communities in 1940 and those links have remained. Even today, the stories of the young evacuees have the power to move us to tears and remind us of the horrors of war.

The links that are already in place between England and Guernsey continue to evolve. Evacuees from Elizabeth College visited Derbyshire in October 2010 to visit their old school premises, and a civic reception was organised for them in Buxton. In 2010, I worked with Peter Trollope of BBC Manchester, on a documentary film which told the story of evacuee Paulette Le Mescam, and her relationship with Eleanor Roosevelt. It was shown on BBC television in England and in the Channel Islands in December 2010. In 2010, the Manchester Beacon for Public Engagement provided the funding for Joanne Fitton and I to interview more evacuees, and to organise an open day in Lancashire. We also created a documentary film with Diane Rickerby, *All my Worldly Possessions: Channel Island Evacuees in Bury and Tottington* which was featured on Channel Islands Television, strengthening the links between Bury and the Channel Islands.[2] In February 2011, Mrs Joan Ozanne and I were jointly presented with the Guernsey Ambassador of the Year Award, which was a great honour. In February 2011, the Stockport and Guernsey Soroptimist associations planted a tree in Guernsey, close to the Evacuation plaque, to mark their enduring links. In May 2011 I organised workshops in several Guernsey primary schools to demonstrate how the child evacuees had adjusted to life in England in 1940. It is hoped that links will be formed between schools in Guernsey and schools England in the near future.

I have set up a Guernsey Evacuee community group which enables me to work on a regular basis with Guernsey evacuees living in Cheshire and Lancashire. Through our group, we share their wartime stories with the community in many different ways, in order to bring their story to life.[3] In October 2011, the Economic & Social Research Council funded a Guernsey Evacuation family event at Stockport's war memorial. BBC television filmed the event, and segments were shown on the BBC in England and in the Channel Islands. In March 2012, our community group took part in the Manchester Histories Festival, and our group and volunteers won a 'Highly Commended' Community Award. In June 2012, the group and I took part in the Bury World War Two Weekend, where our film on Channel Island evacuees in Bury was shown on home ground for the very first time. I am now a volunteer with the Community Archive for Channel Islands Evacuation, in England, which aims to ensure that this story continues to be shared with the public. It is our hope that, at some point, the interviews, photographs and documents collected can be preserved digitally and made available to the general public.

What do these links and commemorations mean to the evacuees themselves? Many now feel that, because there is a plaque to mark the evacuation in Guernsey, their experiences are viewed as an important part of their island's heritage. Geoffrey Heggs stated, 'I am so glad that our stories at last are being told, and that the evacuation is now being marked as an important part of Guernsey's history.' Joan Ozanne told me:

Years ago, I was so frustrated that the story of our evacuation had been overlooked. However, I never imagined that we would have our own plaque!

The evacuees' experiences also form an important part of the story of Britain's Second World War home front. Len Rumens remarked:

It is important that people in Britain, today and in the future, know about Guernsey's history. It was the only part of the British Isles to be occupied and to be evacuated during World War Two, with no chance of a return home until after the war.

Irene Moss believes that children today should understand how the evacuation affected her childhood, and she hopes that such an evacuation will never happen again. Jason Pickering told me the story of his family's evacuation experiences, and then said to me:

I once told a relative who didn't understand what my family had gone through – 'Take this sports bag, and imagine that all you can take is what you can carry in this. Imagine that is all you have. You will be taken to a country you don't know, you will live with people you don't know, and you do not know when you will see your friends and relations and home again. That is what some of my family had to deal with!' My relative then understood that war *isn't* just about soldiers and tanks.

The collection of interviews, together with the archival research, will ensure the preservation of the Guernsey evacuation story for future generations. It is also my sincere hope that my research into the many aspects of this overlooked evacuation, and my efforts to share this story with the public, will continue for years to come.

NOTES

1 The painting is in the care of Stockport Story Museum, while the jug sits in pride of place in Disley Parish Church.
2 The film was also screened at Les Cotils in Guernsey on 7 May 2011, and at Guernsey's 'Sarnia Shorts' festival in October 2012. The DVD can be purchased at: http://guernseyevacuees.wordpress.com/channel-islands-calendar-2011/.
3 See http://guernseyevacuees.wordpress.com/community-project/.

FURTHER READING

Find out more or contact me through my Guernsey research website:
http://guernseyevacuees.wordpress.com/evacuation/

You can also follow me on Twitter: @Guernseyevacuee

Ainger, Lois, *My Case Unpacked*, Guernsey Press, 1995

Allisette, Richard, *Islanders in Kitbags,* Guernsey Press Co. Ltd, 1985

Blicq, Ron, *Au Revoir Sarnia Cherie – Good Bye Dear Guernsey,* RGI International, Canada, 2000

Collenette, Vernon, *Elizabeth College in Exile, 1940–1945*, Guernsey ILS, 1975

Cruickshank, Charles, *The German Occupation of the Channel Islands,* Oxford University Press, 1975

Davidson, Joan, *Evacuated*, Design Innovations, 2005

Le Feuvre, Nellie, *A Sark Teenager's Deportation*, 2005

Hamel, E.J., *X-Isles,* Paramount, Guernsey, 1975

Harris, Roger E., *Islanders Deported Part I: The complete history of those British subjects who were deported from the Channel Islands during the German Occupation of 1940–1945 and imprisoned in Europe*, CISS Publishing, 1980

——, *Islanders Deported Part II: the development and censorship of the Internment Camp Mail Services associated with British subjects deported from the Channel Islands during the German Occupation 1940–1945*, CISS Publishing, 1980 1984

Lang, Suzanne, *Displaced Donkeys: A Guernsey Family's War,* Pinknote Press, New Zealand, 2009

Mawson, Gillian, 'Guernsey Evacuees in the North West of England', *Review of the Guernsey Society*, Winter 2009, Volume LXV, No. 3

——, 'Guernsey Evacuees in Northern England', *BBC History Magazine*, May 2010

——, 'Reliving the heartbreak of wartime evacuation – Guernsey evacuees in Derbyshire during WW2', *Buxton Advertiser*, http://www.buxtonadvertiser.co.uk/features/Reliving-the-heartbreak-of-wartime.5637589.jp

McKenzie, Donald, *The Red Cross Mail Service for Channel Island Civilians, 1940–45*, Picton Publishing, 1975

Molumphy, Henry D., *For Common Decency: the History of Foster Parents Plan 1937–1983*, FPP, Rhode Island, 1984

Le Page, M.J., *A Boy Messenger's War: Memories of Guernsey and Herm 1938–1945*, Arden Publications, St Peter Port, 1995

Le Poidevin, N., *Torteval School in Exile*, Seaflower Books, Jersey, 2010

Le Pelley, P., 'The Evacuation of Guernsey School children', *Channel Islands Occupation Review*, Channel Islands Occupation Society, 1998

Quinn, Olive, *The Long Goodbye: A Guernsey Woman's Story of the Evacuation Years*, Guernsey Press, 1985

Read, Brian Ahier, *No Cause for Panic: Channel Island Refugees 1940–45*, Seaflower Books, 1995

Wood, Alan and Seaton Wood, Mary, *Islands in Danger*, Four Square Books, 1967

Smith, Corral A., *The Impact of the Evacuation and the Occupation Experience, 1940–1945, on the Lives and Relationships of Guernsey Children and Guernsey Society*, Open University, 2005

Tabb, Peter (ed.), *Jersey Evacuees Remember*, Jersey Evacuees Association, 2011

Russell, Yvonne, *A Guernsey Girl Evacuee joins the WAAF in Wartime England*, Toucan Press, Guernsey, 1988

Welshman, John, *Churchill's Children: The Evacuation Experience in Wartime Britain*, Oxford University Press, 2010

Winterflood, Herbert, *Occupied Guernsey 1943–1945: The Final Record*, Guernsey Press, 2002

ACKNOWLEDGEMENTS

My grateful thanks to the following: the evacuees and their families who have shared their wonderful stories and personal documents with me over the past four years. Please be assured that, should your story not be mentioned in this book, it will be used in many other ways, to tell people of all ages about your wartime experiences. I also wish to thank: my family and friends for their never-ending support and encouragement; Michelle Tilling and all at The History Press; Sir Geoffrey Rowland (Bailiff of Guernsey 2005–12) and Lady Diana Rowland; Deputy Mike O'Hara (Minister of Culture and Leisure, Guernsey) and Teresa O'Hara; Mrs Joan Ozanne and her family; Jim Cathcart, and all at BBC Guernsey; Amanda Bennett and all at the Priaulx Library, Guernsey; Darryl Ogier and all at the Island Archives, Guernsey; Di Digard and all at Guernsey Press and the Guiton Group; The March Fitch Fund, who kindly assisted me with research expenses; Joanne Fitton, Leeds University Archives; Joanne Dunn, Sue Shore, Sue Heap and all at Stockport MBC who have worked with me; Dawn Gallienne, Guernsey Post; Michael Paul and the Guernsey Society; Peter Trollope, BBC Television; Raymond Ashton; Donna Hardman, Bury Archive Service; Derek and Gillian Martel; Dot Carruthers, Elizabeth College Archive; The Second World War Experience Centre; Guernsey Retired Teachers Association; Richard Heaume, German Occupation Museum; Renee Holland; Barbara and Mike Mulvihill; Emily McIntosh; Sarah Yorke, UNLtd; The family of the late Maureen Muggeridge; The family of the late Brian Ahier Read; Professor Penny Summerfield; Julie Anderson; Neil Pemberton; Jean Cooper; Ann Barlow; Linne Matthews; Lisa Greenhalgh; Suzanne Spicer; Debra Dickson; Christopher Thorpe; Alice McDonnell; Val Harrington; Fiona Kilpatrick; Rosemary and Robin Wignall; Caroline and Chris Worrall and my colleagues at the University of Manchester. My apologies to those who are not mentioned here, but who are certainly not forgotten!

PRAISE FOR THE AUTHOR

'Gillian's research shows the immense value of oral history for the recovery of histories such as those of the Guernsey evacuees that would disappear from memory altogether were it not for the diligent researcher armed with a voice recorder.'

Professor Penny Summerfield, Professor of Modern History, University of Manchester

'Gillian's book reveals not just an untold evacuation story, but a very unusual one, as the people were moved from a rural island to industrial towns and cities that in many cases became targets for the Luftwaffe's air raids. How they endured that experience and in many cases helped the war effort, despite being far from their homes and families, is something that will fascinate anyone with an interest in history.'

Neil Holmes – *Liverpool Blitzed: Seventy Years On*

'Gillian's use of in-depth personal interviews and wartime diaries gives a wonderful insight into the lives of these "overlooked" evacuees from Guernsey. Readers of all ages will be delighted by this intimate story of thousands of ordinary people who lived through extraordinary circumstances.'

Victoria Aldridge-Washuk – *World War II London Blitz Diary*

'The depth of the research is only surpassed by the informed writing style and passion for the subject.'

John Leete, Historian – http://www.homefronthistory.co.uk/

'In 1945 Channel Islanders left England filled with joy at the prospect of a reunion with their families and friends in Guernsey, but they knew that they had made many friends whom they would never forget and to whom they owed a debt which they would never be able to repay. Gillian's commitment to record the views of Guernsey's evacuees, and to tell the story of their lives in England has been marvellous.'

Sir Geoffrey Rowland, Bailiff of Guernsey 2005–12

'Gillian Mawson's tenacious research and interviews with the Guernsey evacuees allows her to tell this riveting story of war and separation.'

Donald Mounts – Second World War Researcher, USA